Pierce

Six Prairie Lives

Pierce

Six Prairie Lives

A. Mary Murphy

DETSELIG
ENTERPRISES LTD
Calgary, Alberta, Canada

Pierce: Six Prairie Lives © 2010 A. Mary Murphy

Library and Archives Canada Cataloguing in Publication
Murphy, A. Mary (Anne Mary), 1952-
        Pierce : six prairie lives / A. Mary Murphy.
Includes bibliographical references.
ISBN 978-1-55059-403-4

        1. Pierce, Andrew Craig, 1884-1955--Family. 2. Pierce, Margaret Adele,
1882-1961--Family. 3. Pierce family. 4. Alberta--Biography.
I. Title.

CT309.P54M87 2010   929'.20971   C2010-904628-5

Detselig Enterprises, Ltd.   www.temerondetselig.com
210-1220 Kensington Rd NW   temeron@telusplanet.net
Calgary, Alberta, Canada   Phone: 403-283-0900
T2N 3P5   Fax: 403-283-6947

We recognize the support of the government of Canada through the Canada
Books Program for our publishing program.

We also acknowledge the support of the Alberta Foundation for the Arts for our
publishing program.

SAN 113-0234
ISBN 978-1-55059-403-4
Printed in Canada.
Cover design by James Dangerous.
Photo of author by Jenni Shores Photography.

CONTENTS

THE PRAIRIE PEOPLE WHOSE STORIES make up this book are my maternal grandparents and their children. A. Craig Pierce (ACP) is a significant figure in Alberta agriculture, through his farming practice and participation in the Progressive movement between the World Wars. This book also seeks to place him in the midst of his family – his wife Adele (MAM), and their daughters Laura, Hetty, Lucy, and Mary. Because I am part of the family, I have known part of the story all my life, but when I was doing my BA at the University of Lethbridge, I took the opportunity to complete an independent study in History and wrote a twenty-page version that required me to start bringing the pieces together. Ten years later, that beginning grew up to be my doctoral dissertation in English at Memorial University of Newfoundland. This book is an edited version for a wider readership.

Among the many things I wanted to understand when I set out is how each of these six people fit into the shape of this family, and ultimately, I also came to understand a great deal about rural and urban life in Alberta during the early twentieth century. My grandfather was the most public figure in the family, and even within his extended family he still is seen as the centre of that original circle of six. But, I wanted to see each of them more clearly, knowing that all six were equally important in contributing to the family. The women in the house were not as prominent publicly, perhaps, but we all know that the public life is only a part of the whole, and discovering the girls' social lives was a delightful and interesting bonus.

I wanted to make ACP real for myself. This is also true of my grandmother and Laura, my eldest aunt. I have no memory of ACP or Laura and only a few flashes of MAM. In the case of my grandmother, I wanted to find out how she and my grandfather made such a partnership of their marriage, and how she developed as the forceful and opinionated woman I have always perceived her to be. The major interest for me in my aunt's life was the mystery of her health, a mystery that became far more complex as I investigated, and which emerged as a far greater influence on the development of the family than I had imagined. Her early death and her childlessness mean that she has vanished from the family in a physical sense, and that absence is still profoundly felt. Communicating that gap was a central concern.

The last three sisters are part of my own memory. One of them is my mother, and I had anticipated her chapter being the most difficult to write. I was mistaken. Instead, Hetty's was the easiest. Mary's was the most fun. And, I was not prepared for how deeply writing Lucy's story would affect me. I thought I had known these three all my life, but writing their lives required a closer look at their times and circumstances, accepting nothing without closer examination. Understanding and connection, after all, are main reasons any of us reads biography.

My primary sources for this biography were my grandfather's journals, cupboards full of photographs, oral history, and interviews. ACP's journals span 1 January 1919 through 1944 plus 1951–1952 and 1954–1955; in all, his written record of thirty years survives (see appendix A for extracts). Those which have been preserved, in the dark basement at the farm for over half-a-century and now housed and microfilmed at the Glenbow Museum Archive in Calgary, are a wealth of prairie information and a family treasure in themselves. Photograph albums and boxes of loose photographs likewise are safely in the Glenbow collection and are a record of over a century. ACP and MAM lived their married life in Canada, but like many Albertans of the time, they were born and educated in the United Sates, so my research included their regional backgrounds and upbringing.

In the pages of ACP's journals, health symptoms have been diagnosed and illnesses treated, illness ranging from boils to skull fracture to miscarriages; these journals document nephritis, broken arms and feet, sciatica and lumbago, and flu, all with treatments, types of health-care practitioners, the frequency of physician house calls, and occasionally costs of treatment. More explicitly political are the kinds of entries which detail United Farmers of Alberta membership drives and Victory Bond sales and War Services drives and the Progressive movement headed by Premier John Bracken of Manitoba. Anyone interested in the political lobby for fair prices for the prairie farmer during the 1930's will be interested in details recorded in these journals.

Likewise, the journals are a valuable resource for anyone interested in the agricultural milieu as it evolved over three-and-a-half decades, the meteorological data of temperature, rainfall, and wind; production information on strains of grain and their yield, as well as machinery employed. It is the detailed picture of rural men's life written from a male perspective, but the record also includes items of real interest concerning rural women's life. Eventually, Mrs. Phillips came to the farm as cook and stayed for many years, earning $300 per year, the same annual wage as the foreman. Her daily routine is succinctly described during the gruelling pace of spring seeding, serving "breakfast at 5 AM, supper over at 9:15."

When on the farm, ACP recorded every task and who did it, every day: "Crawley pickling, Pierce engine, Codnor drills, Gatine horse drill." The extraordinary weather conditions are consistently recorded: "very windy all day – worst dust storm ever at 6:30 – so dark had lamps lighted. House full of dirt" and "rain in late PM and all night – A life saver." There was "a violent wind and dust storm from the North, looked like a cyclone – dark as night – blew granary into potato patch." The weather record of the journals also shows that life in Alberta took place in a climate that fluctuated from -50 to +100, 150° Fahrenheit in annual range, and an extraordinary 50°F in a winter half-hour.

Whether he was on the farm or in the city, he likewise recorded where everybody in the family went and with whom. ACP was the only one in the house with a driver's licence and was therefore the designated driver as well as the family historian, and in one entertaining sequence, over a matter of days, he drove "Hetty & Lucy to dance at Kirby," "Lucy to Robison's for dance," "Hetty to Rosebud sports & Hymas dance," "Mary to camp," always "shopping" with MAM, and then, helplessly, "all females to different places." There is much in this book to appeal to those with interest in Canadiana, social history, environmental studies, agricultural development, medical history, gender studies, family sociology, economic data, formal education, and prairie heritage – in other words, dating, farming, weather, money, health, school. It's the basic stuff of everyday life.

I remain grateful to my two mentors: Helen M. Buss and E. Roberta Buchanan, whose generous friendship availed me much during my graduate programs. More recently, in the publication of this book, I appreciate very much the financial support of the Alberta Heritage Resources Foundation and the archival support of the Glenbow museum and its staff. I am thankful for the cheerful and efficient efforts of my editor, Aaron Dalton. Throughout, I know my greatest debts are to my aunt, Mary Pierce Conover, who so willingly engaged in many interviews and offered such enthusiastic encouragement for my work; and to my sister, Adele Meyers, who unfailingly urged me on from the start and likes to think about who will play the girls in the movie. I also thank my other interviewees, my mother's cousins Jane Moore Warner and James G. Moore, and the Pierce girls' schoolmate, J. Ken Penley, all of whom talked with me about their memories and helped me understand what the world was like in the years I needed to know. My brothers John Humphries and Craig Humphries shared memories and details, as did my uncle, Gordon Humphries, and my step-father, Mervin Clark, whose agricultural knowledge was called upon many times during this process. My cousins Allison Maus, Laura Dorrans, Mary Sue McLachlan, Candi Taylor, and second-cousin Klaran Warner provided valuable information and photographs for me, as did my cousin Lorne's daughter, Stephanie Jardine.

I am profoundly grateful to the six subjects of this book, my grandparents Adele and Craig Pierce, and their daughters, Laura, Hetty, Lucy, and Mary, to whom all of us in the family are indebted for our sense of history and responsibility, and whose example of abiding love for each other has extended through succeeding generations. It is to them, to my own lovely children, Laura and Benjamin, and my excellent grandchildren, that this work is dedicated.

CHAPTER ONE

THE SOCIAL AND CULTURAL MILIEU

THERE WERE APPROXIMATELY half-a-million people living in Alberta when my grandparents, Craig and Adele Pierce, arrived in 1918. Ninety years later there are a million people living in Calgary alone. The province was just over a decade old and was in a period of rapid internal expansion; the flood of people migrating to the province from all over the world needed schools, hospitals, and transportation and communication infrastructure. Even today, large numbers of Albertans in any census will claim to be born outside the province. Obviously, during the early years of migration into Alberta, the preponderance of residents were born in other places, but before long, Alberta was established as a place of origin, with over half of its residents born in Alberta.[1]

As might be expected, all of this high-speed development resulted in creation of "a high level of public and private debt."[2] At the time, because of its predominantly agricultural demographic, Alberta had a Liberal government that traditionally had a free-trade platform (favoured by farmers over the Conservative preference for high-tariff barriers). Truly free trade was still to the farmers' advantage, but protectionism creates the necessity of subsidies. Once barriers and subsidies are in place on one side of a border, their implementation on the other side becomes a necessary defence. To address the specific concerns of rural people, the United Farmers of Alberta (UFA) was formed by a 1909 merger of two other farmers' organizations, but only in order to lobby government rather than attempt to form government.

The belief among farmers was that they "were over-charged by middle-men for their purchases, and underpaid for their sales of grain, if not cheated."[3] The continuously discouraging level of grain prices might best be explained by the fact that in September 1921, a carload of wheat sold for $1.47 per bushel[4] while the price per bushel in 1992 had risen to only $2. In early 2002, the price was around the $4 mark – it can be a very volatile market, but in this recent case, the increase was a direct result of three consecutive years of drought, creating the irony of high prices for crops which cannot be produced.

A new grain loader cost $575 in 1923[5] and a comparable one cost $4000 in 2002. In other words, the seven-fold increase in the cost of a modest piece of equipment has been paired at best with a less than three-fold increase in the selling price of a bushel of wheat. In 2002, the price tag on a new, average-sized combine was $250 000, and the largest deluxe ones cost the farmer $350 000. Ironically, the industry for which these implements are made and for which they are essential cannot afford to buy them new. Alberta farmers today face the same fundamental cost struggles they faced a century ago.

The province's current status as a petroleum-industry power had its beginnings in 1914 when a Turner Valley well began pumping oil, and agriculture was no longer the sole business in the province. But it was only after the Leduc oil strike in 1947, Alberta's first major strike, that the industry gathered momentum as an economic force, a momentum which continued to build and made Calgary a corporate centre of power. Nevertheless, the national East–West division, which has its origins in agriculture, and is demarcated for Westerners by the Manitoba-Ontario border, has never been overcome and continues to function in Canada. Industry and manufacturing were fostered in central Canada, while raw materials of all kinds were mined and produced in the West.

By logic that defies explanation, Western producers paid the freight for their raw goods to the East and also paid the freight for returning manufactured goods to the West. The Prairies have felt themselves unfairly used since Canada's beginnings when three strokes of the Federal pen – creation of the North-West Mounted Police (NWMP) in

1874 to secure order in the west, negotiation of Treaty 7 with Plains First Nations in 1877 in order to appropriate the land, and establishment of the Canadian Pacific Railway (CPR) in 1881 to move people and goods back and forth across the national expanse – put John A. MacDonald's national vision in motion: populate the West so it can feed the East and buy Eastern goods. Western farmers still feed the country and pay for the privilege of doing so from a population base too small to make any difference in deciding who will occupy 24 Sussex Drive, federal elections being decided before the polls even close in the West.

This imbalance of power and responsibility is the root of Western alienation and the seedbed of Canadian political radicalism, which has been exclusively fostered on the Prairies with the obvious single exception of French-Canadian nationalism. There is not a nationally functioning political party born in Canada that was not born in the Prairies. The "Progressive," which until 2003 was part of the Progressive Conservative Party, comes from the Prairies, as do the New Democratic Party which began as the CCF in 1932 with its founders J. S. Woodsworth of Manitoba and Tommy Douglas of Saskatchewan as its leaders, Social Credit which also was founded in 1932 by Alberta's William Aberhart, and Canadian Alliance which began in Alberta as Preston Manning's Reform Party.

Although historically non-violent, the 1869 Red River Resistance and the 1885 Riel Rebellion notwithstanding, Prairie political activism has nevertheless been highly visible and vigorous. Manitoba was the first Canadian province to extend suffrage to women in 1916 and was followed within months by both Saskatchewan and Alberta. Also in 1916, Alberta appointed the first female magistrate in the British Empire. In 1917, Alberta elected the first women to a legislature in the British Empire, before women even had the right to vote federally. The day after these two women were sworn in, Roberta MacAdams became the first woman to introduce a piece of legislation in the Empire.

In 1921, governments in British Columbia and Alberta appointed the first women as cabinet ministers in the Empire. Three of these "first" women, Alberta's Louise McKinney (MLA), Emily Murphy (Magistrate), and Irene Parlby (Cabinet Minister), launched the renowned Person's Case in 1927, along with two other Alberta women: Nellie McClung (MLA) and Henrietta Muir Edwards, co-founder of the National Council of Women. Women had been persons legally in Alberta since 1917, but in 1929 the so-called Famous Five won their case, not in Canada's Supreme Court, which had found against the plaintiff, but in their subsequent appeal to the British Privy Council, and thus women throughout the British Empire became persons under the law.

Predictably, these political activists were from the ranks of reformer parties, with the exception of Nellie McClung who was elected to the Alberta Legislature in 1921 as a Liberal opposition member. The political affiliations of Roberta MacAdams and Louise McKinney were with the Non-Partisan League, a group concerned with issues and not party allegiances or policies, when they were elected in 1917. Irene Parlby was a UFA candidate in the 1921 Alberta provincial election. Parlby was also president of the United Farm Women of Alberta. Another group organized among rural women was the Alberta Women's Institute, established in 1909 and expanding to two-hundred-twelve branches by 1917.[6] Although perhaps it is true that "Women's Institutes were more about housekeeping and had less interest and involvement in political affairs than the UFWA,"[7] it is important to acknowledge the contribution of Women's Institutes (WI) on a variety of women's issues.

On a very basic level, WI meetings, held in private homes throughout farming communities and which I know from my childhood, created a network of survival for a group of women who found themselves socially and intellectually isolated. Aside from accomplishing the very necessary social function of its regular gatherings, WI agendas included talk about health care, education, the Dower law (to create a wife's legal right to her husband's property acquired during marriage and to prevent a husband's disinheriting his wife), and other politically important topics of concern to women. On the practical side, the organization established "rest rooms" in towns, places where farm women could go to refresh themselves and their children during their occasional trips to town for shopping. At the same time, however, in spite of enormous progress, women still had to deal with the prevailing attitude of men such as that of the Vice-Principal Academic at Western Canada High School, who wrote in his 1936 address to the students that "Good pies will do much more to further happiness in a home than the knowledge of Latin or trigonometry."[8]

The UFA, itself having been formed from two other groups, merged with the Alberta Non-Partisan League in 1919 (the year of organized labour's six-week Winnipeg General Strike which made news headlines around the world) and became part of the national Progressive movement. My grandfather spent several days in 1920 recruiting members for the UFA. After World War I, commodity prices for farm products dropped while production costs increased. The Progressives sought the removal of import duties on manufactured items and the lowering of freight rates for agricultural produce. The feeling among those involved with agriculture was and is that Canada's founding political parties would always privilege corporate interests in Ontario and Quebec and never concern itself overmuch with farmers' issues in Alberta, Saskatchewan, and Manitoba.

The Progressive movement sought to break the grip of party politics, instead advancing the concept of a "delegate democracy wherein those elected to Parliament would voice the concerns of their constituents without an obligation to support a political party."[9] Clearly, this dream has never seen more than a glimpse of fruition. Members of Parliament are still expected and pressured, by party Whips no less, to support their party's line and are seldom freed to vote according to conscience. Progressive ideology led to the provincial election victory of the United Farmers of Ontario in 1919, the United Farmers of Alberta in 1921, and the United Farmers of Manitoba in 1922.

The Alberta UFA government quickly created the Alberta Wheat Pool in 1923, with a mandate of "orderly marketing."[10] The Pool made partial payment to farmers on delivery of their grain to the elevator, and full payment was calculated after the grain was sold. This partial-payment practice not only put money in the farmers' pockets sooner, and therefore gave them expendable income sooner, but the strategy also meant that the price paid in the end was based on the market and went to the farmer instead of to traders profiting from speculation on the Grain Exchange.

Regrettably but inevitably, the UFA began to function as a traditional party rather than as a delegate democracy because it was functioning within a structure devised for the practice of party politics. Without fundamental changes to the framework, that framework over time will force those within it into compliance with its form. The UFA elected a Calgary lawyer as its leader, rather than a farmer, and as a party rather than a movement it still managed to win two more elections in 1926 and 1930 but with a smaller majority each time. However, wheat prices had begun to drop in 1929 and the Depression was underway. As a result, "There was only one government in Canada, provincial or dominion, to survive a Depression election – that of [Progressive leader] John Bracken of Manitoba in 1932 (and again in 1936) – and it was a coalition."[11]

Prairie farmers were in the midst of a combined economic and environmental catastrophe, and urban unemployment in Alberta was at 25%, so the financial situation was ripe for someone with a convincing plan for fiscal recovery. Calgary high school principal and radio evangelist William (familiarly known as "Bible Bill") Aberhart, like many others, had read and embraced C. H. Douglas' economic theory known as Social Credit. The basic premise is that there is not enough money in circulation to buy everything that is available to be bought. Interpretation lay in what to do about this fact, and part of Aberhart's plan was for government to pay every adult Albertan a non-currency purchasing power of $25 per month, a substantial sum in the Dirty Thirties. This was a popular plan. Still, regardless of its popularity, no standing party would incorporate the concept into its platform, and Aberhart, who had wanted to expedite change without formally entering politics, discovered that if he wanted his plan implemented he would have to do it himself.

Alberta Social Credit was born, and although it would never exactly carry out its foundational policy, it would form the government in Alberta from 1935 to 1971. When its candidates won the 1935 election, they were a leaderless caucus initially because Aberhart had not run, but one of them stepped aside to facilitate Aberhart's entry into the Legislature via by-election, and reluctantly, he officially entered the world of party politics. During the next several years, Social Credit enacted a wide range of Acts directed at wages, debt control, taxation, licensing, and price control, all of which demonstrated that "in a social credit system, production and distribution are to be communal matters regulated by the government".[12] As its name might imply, Social Credit has a distinct socialist flavour, although some "described [certain of the government's policies] as fascist."[13] Its policies did not find favour in Calgary's exclusive Mount Royal district where only 20% of the vote was cast for Social Credit in 1935, whereas it received 68% among the working class in other regions of the city.[14]

A WI report on the development in Alberta's farmhouses in the early 1940's indicates that

> only 55% have electric light, 4.3% have bathrooms, 2.5% have flush toilets, 17.17% have a refrigerator, 18.1% have a telephone, 1.9% have a vacuum cleaner, only 10% have furnace heating and 57% are heated with wood.[15]

On almost all of these points ("almost all" of them only because the dates when refrigeration and vacuum cleaners were purchased are unknown), the house on the Pierce farm at Drumheller was well ahead of the average in the addition of modern conveniences. It had a telephone listing for the first time in 1922. In June 1925, the house was optimistically busy with plumbers and "light wiring men,"[16] but commercial electricity did not come to the farm until late 1948 when the Canadian Utilities Company ran an experimental line ten miles from Drumheller out along the highway to a point just south past the farm.

Calgary had had electrical power since 1887, although of course not for everyone and not all the time because it was a luxury; when power came to smaller communities, they had electricity provided for perhaps two or three hours once or twice each day. However, while they waited for utilities to reach them, some farmers had their own wind-charged 32-volt batteries, and ACP (my grandfather) was one of those. My eldest brother explains

> There was a wind charger in the yard to the NE of the house and the battery room was in what is now the upstairs bathroom. In there, there were square or rectangular shaped glass jars and the wires used to run from the charger into the jars (one wire into the first jar and then from there on from jar to jar). There was a whole mess of them and they were all hooked up in series.

The gallon jars were the batteries and were full of acid. Eventually the battery room was renovated into a roomy full bathroom. The plumbing installed in 1925 was for the main floor and eventually serviced a tiny corner space requisitioned from the pantry to install a sink and toilet. A "pipeless furnace" was purchased at the Marshall Wells store in Drumheller and installed in the cellar during the first week of November 1940[17]; "furnace control chains" were used to open or close the draft in order to create more or less burn. The chains could be installed in order to be controlled from the main floor, approximating the function of a thermostat. The "ventilator from living room over furnace to kid's bedroom"[18] was installed later in November 1942.

The house was heated with coal until the late 1950's when a forced-air oil furnace replaced the coal heat that had circulated up through floor grates my siblings and I knew as children. Our grandfather's eagerness to upgrade things notwithstanding, in some cases acquisition of improvements could not be hastened no matter how innovative the householder: if there are no telephone lines in the district, a telephone in the house is a pointless embellishment. Other things, such as plumbing and wind generators, required a combination of money and a progressive attitude.

By the time the Pierces acquired a permanent city residence, Calgary had a streetcar system (established 1909), a library (1912), a radio station (1922), five hospitals (1890–1926), the Provincial Institute of Technology (1916), Alberta College of Art (1926), and at least seven movie theatres. Since its incorporation as a town in 1884, Calgary has experienced spectacular population growth.[19] Throughout the twentieth century, almost every decade saw a population increase of at least one-third. During the hard economic years of the Depression and the 1980's, population growth was only around 6%.

Although it will never equal the 960% increase of the first decade of the twentieth century, Calgary still added approximately 200 000 people in the last decade of the century. It is a cosmopolitan city, known for its high energy that never seems to wane. Its attractiveness as a place to which so many wish to relocate means that it continues to have all the same logistical issues of rapid population growth, combined with the need for infrastructure to support that growth. Ironically, in spite of abundant evidence to the contrary, Calgary and the West in general continue to be perceived by many as a vast backwater inferior in every way to central Canada. As Canada is in the contemporary American mind, mired in a combined lack of knowledge and attitude of superiority, so is the West to the East within Canada.

City living in Calgary's Mount Royal was a completely different kind of life from life on the farm. This prestigious section of the city is where, after ten years of rental accommodation for winter residence, Craig and Adele Pierce decided to buy a city home. It was their permanent address from late 1928 until the family unit began to disperse as the girls married or went to college. The house on the corner at 1223 19th Avenue West, had crystal door-knobs, front and back stairs up to the second floor, and a fireplace in the master bedroom,

The Pierce house at 1223 19th Ave

where "the privilege of the sick was to be put in mother's bedroom."[20] The house on the corner is no longer there. None of the three houses the Pierces occupied after the girls started school is still standing, as Calgary constantly concerns itself far more with expansion than preservation.

Nineteenth Avenue is called Cameron Avenue now, and the house on the corner has been replaced by a condominium: where one family lived, there is now space for many. Almost all of the houses on 19th Avenue are no longer there. On the north side are 1960's brick apartment buildings and on the south side are the 1990's idea of beautiful living, what Mary Pierce Conover describes as "some damn modern thing."[21] The streets are still winding and narrow, and the trees are still mature, but progress has been here and wiped out the grace that used to be lower Mount Royal. The primary motive for maintaining a year-round city residence was the issue of the girls' schooling.

By the fall of 1928, they were aged twelve, ten, eight, and seven and already had been schooled in the city for two years. The elder three had begun schooling at Kirby school in the country, but "there was no way in hell [their] folks were going to allow [them] to be educated in a one-

Kirby School on a Sunday

Cliff Bungalow School

room school."[22] The school was located approximately five miles from the farm and doubled as the community's church, with local men taking turns leading the service. Laura had completed grades one through three at Kirby, and Hetty and Lucy had each completed grade one there. For the first two years that the girls were in the Calgary School Board system, the family rented a house at 1929 5A Street West; while there, Laura attended Earl Grey (eight blocks from home), and Hetty and Lucy were at Cliff Bungalow (only two-blocks walk) for one year. Both schools were located in Mount Royal; Cliff Bungalow is still open but operates as a Montessori school.

By the time Mary started grade one in 1927, all four girls were at Earl Grey. Following the move to 1223, the girls were sent to Mount Royal School only five blocks from home until they each completed grade eight and had to attend King Edward School sixteen blocks away for grade nine before they went on to Western Canada High School. Mary admits "actually [her] mother was a snob," who "was upset when [they] had to go to King Edward [elementary-junior high school] [. . .] because [they] had to go to school with the riff raff."[23] After all, King Edward was two blocks over on the west side, the wrong side, of 14th Street, meaning it was not in Mount Royal. All of the other schools the girls attended in Calgary were located in a very small and very upper class area. If their mother could have wielded any influence to circumvent this ruling, she

King Edward School

most certainly would have, but the Pierces were not yet prominent enough in the city to have matters of this sort handled for them.

Drumheller was a different story, and ACP apparently made significant use there of his personal influence at about this same time on behalf of his nephew Joseph Audley Pierce, Jr., in January 1929. Junior had arrived from Pittsburgh the previous summer, ostensibly to work on the farm for the season and return home. However, he remained in Canada through the fall and committed a substantial robbery at the Alexandra Hotel in Drumheller. The front page newspaper account in *The Drumheller Mail*[24] refers to him as a "Pittsburgh college student" who had come to work in the area during harvest and then been employed at some unnamed job in town, but without explanation as to why he was in Alberta and not in Pennsylvania midway through the academic year. Indeed, there is no known explanation for this since ACP's journals offer none, and no one remembers.

He earned $2 a day plus room and board for twenty-four days of harvesting in September and then disappeared from the journal record. The lack of any mention of Junior from October to December 1928, when he was still in the near vicinity, is suggestive of something, certainly, but it is impossible to know exactly what. The paper reported that, "being out of employment and short of money, he succumbed to temptation."[25] The paper does what no newspaper, no matter how reputable or disreputable, would consider doing now, making no mention of what everyone in town undoubtedly knew: the defendant was Craig Pierce's nephew.

Clearly, the unemployed-and-out-of-cash angle quite simply was less than the whole truth. Junior's agreement to plead guilty, make restitution of the $200 theft, and leave the country "to go back to his parents immediately"[26] in exchange for suspension of his twelve-month sentence, could only have been accomplished through his uncle's influence. If he'd been a less noteworthy local person's nephew, he would have served his year in jail and then likely have been deported. As it was, two days after conclusion of his trial on January 8th, ACP escorted him by train all the way home to Pennsylvania.[27] On the same day the report appeared in the paper, Junior left Calgary for good. His father met them at the station in Pittsburgh on the 13th, and we can assume it was a rather grim homecoming. ACP visited with his family for a few days and returned home to Calgary having done his duty to his older brother by keeping his only son out of jail.

For the next dozen years, the Pierce girls lived relatively unaware of the degree to which they were privileged people. More than once they remarked that the Depression had no real effect on them, although they did recall men coming to the back door asking for a meal in exchange for carrying out some small task. Both Hetty and Mary said that their mother never sent a man away unfed. Almost certainly the girls were sheltered so far as possible from the financial impact of the worldwide depression which was compounded by the dismal agricultural conditions of the Dirty Thirties. However, while they were spared the fears and losses experienced by so many on the prairies, there had to be measurable financial realities which impacted their lives. Mary said "the only thing I recall about the Depression was I wanted a bike and we couldn't afford a bike and then I got a bike. [...] I did not feel it. I don't recall the bread lines."[28]

The Mount Royal house was bought on the eve of the stock market crash of 1929, amid seemingly stable economic times where farming expenses and income were increasing at a roughly equivalent rate. There was "relative prosperity on the prairies in the late 1920s – based on good, stable grain prices and above average yields,"[29] and perhaps fiscal prudence during that decade helped somewhat to minimize the potential for disaster when the sudden and dramatic change came. An earlier period of strife, when "the price of wheat, which had stood at $2.82/bushel in September 1920, had suffered a long, frightening slide to $1.11/bushel in December 1921,"[30] showed how uncertain a market there was for grain, and the memory would not have faded although security had returned. Prices for agricultural products and prices paid for manufactured goods were nearly the same ratio in 1926 as they had been in 1913. However, "at harvest time, 1930, a common grade of wheat sold for $1.40 per bushel, but by early spring 1931, the price had dropped to 40 cents, dropping further to a low of 16 cents."[31] This mathematical reality "caused the net income per farm in Alberta to drop from $1,975 in 1927 to only $54 in 1933."[32]

Mary recalled that their mother "was very frugal,"[33] but the Pierces made only personal use of their non-grain farm products in the city. They did not sell garden produce, meat, or dairy products out the back door. Mary related the story of how

> Daddy would come in from the farm on Friday night [. . .] and bring [. . .] milk and cream and [there would be] a hundred million at least of glass quarts and a funnel and my mother would scald them.[34]

Adele would make and sell doughnuts, but that money was donated to Wesley United Church.[35] The impact of any economic stressors there may have been was absorbed by the parents, allowing the girls to remain blissfully untroubled by uncertainty. Hetty said she knew at the time things were difficult for others, but that it really did not affect them. Insulated from real deprivations by virtue of family money on both sides (though not enormous wealth) and an upper-class neighbourhood, "The Pierce Girls," as they were known, enjoyed the 1930s, strange as it may sound.

The girls "didn't even make [their] own beds [. . . but] Thursday was the maid's day off – then [they] had to do the dishes."[36] They attended Western Canada High School, which according to the school yearbook, by 1939 had a staff of fifty and over fifteen-hundred students and was the largest school in western Canada.[37] It also was located in lower Mount Royal and "as close as you came to private school,"[38] where the entire academic-student population was as privileged and white as they were. The school had no written dress code because it had no need for one. The students just dressed in a certain way. "The boys wouldn't dress casually [. . .] shirts and ties and suits [. . .] not everybody but an awful lot," and those who did not wear suits wore a "shirt and tie and sweater."[39] In 1937, Dunn's Tailors sold suits and coats, made only of "All British Woolens," for $15.95, $18.95, and $21.95.[40]

Western Canada was strictly an academic institution until 1935–36 when the school began offering technical courses, such as cooking, sewing, metals, woods, and electricity. Because of their uniqueness, the technical programmes drew students from all over the city, but the academic programmes remained strictly regional.[41] Mary remembered no people of colour whatsoever, but the yearbooks spanning the five years (1934–39) when the Pierce girls were students there do have one or two non-European faces, the children of prosperous Asian business people. Calgary was a very white city at the time, and although it remains so

Western Canada High School

today, two generations later, when compared with much larger Canadian urban centres, the city has a vigorous ethnic and racial mix.

During the 1930s, the school paper included the occasional racist reference, such as one about "not-too-bright Eskimos [. . . and] North American Indian[s]" in a so-called humour piece on the correlation between intelligence and high brows, easily disproved by the so-called fact that "Eskimos" and "Indians" have the highest foreheads on earth.[42] The picture of an extraordinary racial imbalance at the time, the school at the turn of the twenty-first century had become a very broadly diverse racial community with an equally mixed class representation drawn from high-performing academic students across the city.

None of the Pierce girls ever indicated that either of their parents led them to believe they were racially superior to any other people, all the hired household help were white and "treated like family,"[43] but they lived in a world with built-in structures of apartness pertaining to race and class. ACP's college fraternity, for example, had no issues of race at the time he joined because "When Phi Delta Theta was founded college men were mostly of one race, creed and color,"[44] so exclusionary policies were moot. However, "a century later the college population was as varied as the census [. . .] and [American] west coast chapters became concerned about the membership of Orientals"[45]; those chapters passed racist resolutions in 1910 and 1912.

In the mid-1950s, those same chapters were thoroughly pressed (on threat of losing their campus charters) to rescind these rules and so complied at the 1956 General Convention, strategically wording their new membership restriction which "eliminates any reference to race, color or creed but stipulates [. . .] all members [. . .] must be acceptable to *all* chapters,"[46] thus deftly circumventing university regulations and maintaining in practice their exclusive membership rolls by saying it without literally saying it. There is no source of information to indicate what Craig Pierce had to say about this issue which was of specific relevance to him.

While he did not end his association (on the contrary, far from it) with the fraternity on the basis of this "Knotty Question,"[47] he was a member of the non-exclusive Renfrew Club in Calgary, where he played bridge with Mr. Goldberg,[48] who also would have been a member. Since he once also harboured bootleggers overnight in 1919,[49] he apparently did not embrace all of the attitudes of his rather temperate and racist fraternal organization. Rather, he lived in the world and that was the way of the world. Just as "a widespread fraternity exists in the stream of life, and the currents of history flow through and around it,"[50] so those currents flowed around him. Admittedly, this sparse information does not satisfy, and some more explicit statement of his thinking is much to be desired, but not to be found.

The most awkward piece of evidence on the issue of race that exists for the Pierces is in a letter Laura wrote at the age of eleven to her mother, in which she writes of their cat "Niger." It took several readings before realization dawned on my temporal distance: my assumption that this was a clever naming of a cat after the African river was mistaken, and that far more likely this is a misspelling on the girl's part, that the undoubtedly black cat was named "Nigger." Mary was unable to confirm this because she does not remember the cat, although she thinks there was a workhorse on the farm named "Nig."

Unfortunately, this sparse information is everything available to me that addresses issues of race, including the question of lands, rights, and perceptions of Prairie Aboriginal peoples, and disappointingly does not allow for any conclusion beyond an unhappy acceptance that here is an example of unconscious malice, the kind of social practice in which people engage as a result of unexamined cultural norms, a passive, received racism. However, in this household, based on the daughters' recollections, social class does seem to have been a far greater concern than race, and that for Adele far more than for Craig. This is consistent with Alberta itself, which is far more classist than racist. Financial prosperity is the first measure of a person here, a measure that has its roots in the Protestant work ethic, and race is a secondary measure.

Neither of these issues had any bearing on the girls' social lives, since no one of difference ever entered their sphere. All of their dates came for them by car, never on foot, and never by streetcar.[51] They always went to the very regular dances at Penley's Academy, "formal big dances"[52] sponsored not by the school but by any of the various clubs and fraternities or sororities at school. It would "never occur to [them] not to be going."[53] Some of the social rules included the fact that "Girls couldn't go without dates, even groups of girls. Frequently [they'd] have corsages [. . .] and a long dress. Fellas just wore suits."[54] The girls could get a $2.50 student special at Locke's Permanent Wave Shoppe, or other waves for up to $6.50, and if they needed a hat they could pop into the Darling Hat Shop for "The Smartest in Millinery" with prices ranging from just $1.88 to $4.88.[55]

For the price of "50 cents per couple," the dances featured an orchestra, perhaps "Larry Seville's [. . .] 'Hi-Hatters,'"[56] never recordings, and sometimes with a singer, and refreshments downstairs at intermission. Did they have dance cards? "Oh gosh yes." These were formal, printed cards, and each evening had a set number of dances. The rule was that a girl danced at least the first and last dances with her date and also spent the intermission in his company. If another boy wanted to ask a girl to dance, he first had to ask her date for permission to ask her. If the date was agreeable, the girl then could be asked, but she did not feel compelled to accept even though her escort would allow it.[57]

The orchestra would have played Artie Shaw tunes (once Shaw "overthrew Benny Goodman to become the popular leader of the thousands of jitterbugs and swing fans"), Jack Leonard songs with Tommy Dorsey's band, Bing Crosby of course, and Ella Fitzgerald.[58] The songs would have included covers of Rudy Vallee's "Vieni Vieni," and other songs with the trend of "foreign titles," such as "Ti-pi-tin" and "Bei Mir Bist Du Schoen," and "beautiful Scottish lyrics were caught in the swing-man's noose [. . .] 'Loch Lomond' and [. . .] 'Swingin' Through the Rye.'"[59] When they danced,

> The dignified waltz and the customary fox-trot were shelved, to be replaced by a bedlamish combination of a gymnastic display and nature in the raw [. . .] crazy hooting

crowds [. . .] hopped, skipped and jumped around Penley's and St. Mark's yelling, 'Praise Allah!' and 'Truck in behind!' [. . .] the names of the alleged dance steps that made up the miscellaneous collection known as the 'Big Apple' [. . .] were: truckin', shaggin', Susie Q., peckin', and posin'.[60]

Penley's School of Dance was on 8th Avenue, west of Eaton's. After the dance, in the tradition of dating youth, they'd go to a favourite spot, such as a café. "On 4th Street [which is still a major restaurant strip] there was a place. It was all counters and of course a big Wurlitzer [juke box] and we'd always go there after Penley's."[61] Students at Western Canada also had after-school dances, called "Lits" (no one could tell me why), which would run for an hour or so, starting at 4 o'clock. As with the dances at Penley's, Lits would be sponsored by student groups. This "sock-hop" type gathering was not exclusive to Western Canada High School, but Crescent Heights High School never hosted a dance.

William Aberhart was principal there from 1915–1935, before his political career made him Premier of Alberta, and exercised such rigid control over his students' social lives that he even dictated how they spent their off-campus, out-of-school hours. Ken Penley remembered a Crescent Heights boy who formed a band with his friends and played at Penley's one night.

On the next day of school, Aberhart summoned the boy to his office where the young musician was "threatened with expulsion"[62] – and the band never played again. Aberhart was "associated with a number of fundamentalist churches before he and his colleagues established the Calgary Prophetic Bible Institute in 1927,"[63] and although not ordained, Aberhart did preach in churches on a pulpit relief basis. He also had a weekly evangelistic radio broadcast starting in 1925 and continuing even after his election – a conflict which would be unacceptable in today's political climate. The broad audience appeal of the programme and of Aberhart's personal style meant there was a ready-made network prepared and attentive when Aberhart began to promote Social Credit theory over the air. Northern Alberta, however, did not have radio reception for the programme, and Social Credit's share of the popular vote there was correlatively low.[64]

In contrast to those governed by Principal Aberhart, there were no edicts against dancing and social activities for Laura, Hetty, Lucy, and Mary. The Pierce girls never had a curfew, never went straight home after a dance, and in fact would have been "mad if [they] did."[65] "Sometimes [they'd] go park – but [they] were very pure."[66] Mary insists that kissing was the limit of these parking interludes, and that no boy ever even attempted to touch her "below the neck":

> Nobody had sex with anybody – no no no no no [. . .] I had lots and lots and lots and lots of boyfriends but nobody ever laid a glove on me – ever – he didn't even try – and we used to do a lot of parking but there was never any of this back-seat stuff [. . .] It did not exist [. . .] We didn't drink either – no drinking and no sex and no attempt at sex.[67]

Casual sex "did not exist" to such an extent that their parents never talked to them about it. Mary admits that there were "fast girls," and when one "went to get her appendix out [they'd] think 'hmmm.'"[68] Their mother told the Pierce girls she trusted them, even when they "were out until all hours [. . . and] were every direction, driving in cars, going to dances, [. . . she] trusted [them] – sometimes with fear and trembling, but [she] trusted [them],"[69] and of course she knew all their friends. This was the mother's territory and their father "didn't butt into [their] social lives."[70]

Just as the Depression and date sex "did not exist," neither did homosexuality. Mary recalls one boy at school who

> to the best of [her] knowledge was the only gay person [they] knew [. . .] Gay hadn't been invented yet [. . .] [He] was effeminate – that's all [. . .], but in retrospect [she] [didn't] think at the time that [they] thought he was gay or whatever [. . .] No, [they] just thought he was effeminate – *real*.[71]

Apparently, this young man benefited from the general ignorance of his schoolmates in that he was not harassed. Since "gay hadn't been invented yet," neither had gay bashing – at least not within this very limited scope. To Mary's knowledge, no one ever beat him up or gave him any trouble for his difference. To the list of descriptors "white" and "privileged," add "straight." Everyone was heterosexual, so much so that the term had no purpose.

During their high school years, the two younger girls were in a state of constant social motion. The norm was for groups of friends to plan activities together. Many Sunday evenings would find "twenty-five boys and maybe five girls, maybe just Lucy and [Mary] and [their friend] Margaret"[72] at the Pierce house. Craig and Adele would be out playing bridge, and at home "Gord Humphries [whose brother married my mother] would be playing the piano and [they'd] dance and [Mary] remember[ed] sitting around the dining room table playing cards."[73] Craig and Adele would call promptly at ten o'clock, just before heading home themselves, to tell the girls it was time to break up the party.

Craig and Adele's social set was drawn primarily from the ranks of Craig's business contacts; the husbands of many of the couples with whom they associated had offices in the Lancaster Building, downtown on the corner of 8th Avenue and 2nd Street. The ten-storey sandstone brick building housed lawyers, accountants, insurance agents, grain-trade companies, and various energy-resource companies, and was located near the Grain Exchange building. The Lancaster listings in *Henderson's Calgary Directory* show it to be a convenient one-stop industry and commerce hub, where a man could walk the halls and find an office door lettered with the name of someone in whatever profession or occupation he found himself in need, and consequently also encounter an addition to the social life of his family.

In this community of the prosperous the parents socialized with whomever the husband conducted his business, and their children all attended the same school and the same parties. There is no question that the Pierce girls were immensely popular. The high school yearbooks and newspapers clearly support the image Mary paints of the younger girls as the focal point of the "innest" crowd there was. For the academic year 1937/38 there are only six issues of the weekly *Western Mirror* that mention neither Lucy nor Mary. Laura and Hetty, though, did not have a role in this social whirl; the older sisters were, for different reasons, moving in a less carefree and heady round of events.

And soon, they all were. Saturday nights spent "hanging on the radio [...] for the Hit Parade"[74] came to a dramatic halt at the end of August 1939. These friends spent the first night of World War II all together, stayed up all night at a friend's house, "and the next day all the guys went out and enlisted"; "[the girls] went to college and they went to war. Everybody went to war."[75] All my uncles went to war.

R. Gordon Humphries

Lorne S. McMurchy

Henry M. Conover

James J. Jardine, Jr.

CHAPTER TWO

MARGARET ADELE MOORE PIERCE (1882–1961)

MAM WAS BORN IN 1882 IN THE bituminous-coal country along the Allegheny Plateau of south-western Pennsylvania, where her father was general manager of the River View Coal Mining Company. Her birthplace was a quasi-town called Catfish Camp, located along a tributary of Catfish Creek that, according to local tourism brochures, was "the first county created after the signing of the Declaration of Independence" and was "the only county established during the Revolution." The town was "originally the village of Delaware native-American chief Tingoocqua, who had been nicknamed 'Chief Catfish.'"

The comparatively unworldly Catfish Camp had three successive locations all in what is now the town site of Washington, Pennsylvania, located about twenty miles south from the outskirts of modern-day Pittsburgh: Sharls' Farm, Allison Avenue, and the present location of the Immaculate Conception Roman Catholic Church. At some point, the Moore family moved to Kittanning on the Allegheny River (where Dellie's, as MAM was sometimes called, parents had been married), eighty miles to the northeast of Washington, but relocated to Buffalo in 1890 when she was eight. Her dearest friendship, with Lucy Allen, for whom she would name her third daughter, was formed during her years in Buffalo. Lucy became a photographer and later married Frank Sipprell, a moderately renowned photographic-portraitist who would later make many of the photographs of Adele and particularly of her children. Lamentably, there is no trace of any letters Adele undoubtedly wrote to describe her life in the West to her best friend.

The Moores lived in a large three-storey frame house at 618 Richmond Avenue, a broad street bordered by house after enormous house with hitching posts along the street for carriage horses, but they summered in a bungalow at 9 Hurst Avenue in Chautauqua. These houses survive but have long been out of the family. A few blocks from the Richmond Avenue house is the imposing, dark-red brick United Methodist Episcopal Church with its beautiful rose window, where the family would have attended services. The Chautauqua house with its low-roofed veranda and leaded-glass windows now seems located in a time capsule along the narrow, winding, tree-lined streets, planned for horses rather than automobiles, on the shores of Lake Chautauqua.

In the full summer shade of those trees, the town is now a cultural centre and enjoys summers of intellectual and artistic lectures, courses, and performances which have made the name Chautauqua so well known. The houses are rented for the season by the privileged few who can afford the leisure to enrich themselves for months at a time in peaceful (almost carless) surroundings. This house was built by the family and is the only survivor of three matching homes. The other two were located side-by-side on Water Street by the Allegheny River in Kittanning (one hundred miles south of Chautauqua) and were the homes of Dellie's maternal cousins. The Chautauqua house is where Dellie awaited the births of her first and last children.

She lived on Richmond Avenue until 1898 when she was sixteen, during which time her brother Mac was at Yale, while Al and Arthur, the two elder brothers, were established in their banking and coal-executive careers. Then she returned to Washington for four years as a boarding student at the Washington Female Seminary, serendipitously located on Maiden Street. The school was established in 1835 when "a number of prominent men in the town, who wished to begin a school for the advanced education of their daughters, met at the home of Congressman McKennan."[1] The buildings were three storeys and included forty lodging rooms[2]; approximately one quarter of the one-hundred-forty-member student body were boarders[3] and most of the rooms accommodated two pupils, but were furnished with single beds.[4]

Applications to the boarding department had to be "accompanied by suitable references,"[5] and parents were "requested to furnish the Principals with lists of the persons with whom they [were] willing to have their daughters correspond."[6] When Adele entered the Seminary, its education buildings were brand new: "Roman Classic in design, of vitrified brick with moulded brick trimmings."[7] Graduates of the college preparatory programme were guaranteed admission to the Freshman class at Vassar,[8] but Adele registered in that stream for only her first year.[9] Her remaining three years were not academically less demanding, however.

Of Adele's class of thirty-four students who were together for three years of the programme, twenty-one completed the fourth year and graduated.[10] Adele's grades are unavailable, but she did graduate; her diploma is dated 3 June 1902, and the calendar sternly warns "that it should be clearly understood [. . .] that a certificate [would] be given by the school only for work which [was] thoroughly satisfactory."[11] The Regular Course served to "give mental discipline and culture to students who [did] not intend to pursue their studies further."[12] This was not a school for "finishing" and teaching young ladies the domestic arts; they were not taught how to look after husbands and families. On the contrary, the prospectus expressly states that domestic things such as "dressmaking [. . .] should be attended to at home, as [it took] the time of the pupils from recreation and study."[13]

The seminary prospectus outlines a daily regimen that began with breakfast at 7:00, ended with the "Retiring bell" at 9:30, and included a substantial two hours of "Physical culture and out-door exercise."[14] Aside from bath and bed linens, girls were expected to bring from home "six table napkins and napkin ring," "spoon, knife and plate for personal use in room," and a "linen scarf for bureau and washstand."[15] The prospectus also contains the caution that, "As a matter of good taste we recommend the strictest simplicity in dress and ornaments. Low-necked and sleeve-less gowns are not suitable for school girls."[16] The fees schedule indicates that basic "board with furnished room, light, heat, washing (one dozen garments per week) and Tuition in English, Latin, Greek, French, German and Scientific Studies" were billed at $300 per year plus an additional $75 per year for girls enrolled in the Regular or College Preparatory Departments.[17] Additional fees were levied for extra-academic accomplishments such as those offered to students enrolled in Music and Art.

The Seminary's Home Department's goal was to attend to the "health, character and general culture of pupils [. . .] [and] to develop in students the power of self-control and self-government."[18] The prospectus promises that dormitory life "[was] made home-like and the restrictions imposed [were] only such as [were] necessary for the welfare and comfort of all."[19] Nevertheless, "No pupil [was] retained who [was] unable to adapt herself to the requirements of the school."[20] The girls from Washington Female Seminary would be at least as well-equipped with an intellectual confidence for their lives as they were for the domestic realm by their training at home. These young women left school firmly aware that they were thinking women with sufficient formal preparation to engage in conversation with formally educated men and women.

Perhaps this is a contributing factor to Adele's remaining single for many years after her graduation. The family story is that "she was having too much fun to get married." No doubt it is more complicated than that, but the statement has a basic truth to it. Adele remained unmarried for thirteen years after leaving the seminary. She was beautiful, socially more than acceptable, and had many courtship opportunities. Of special worth in American social standing is the military connection of the family. MAM was, in her own words, "descended from the Revolution,"[21] and was in fact a member of the Daughters of the American Revolution. Her father had served the Union under Sherman, Burnsides, and Grant in the Civil War, was present at Lee's surrender, and had been wounded at South Mountain. Her photo album records casual daytime outings with mixed groups of friends and has enough snapshots of two young men in particular as to make it likely they were serious contenders for her hand. They were both students at Cornell University in Ithaca, located on the tip of one of the Finger Lakes in central New York State, and so may have been Buffalo boys.

Adele's photo album, acquired in July 1902, is not entirely trustworthy because there is some year hopping in the arrangement of the photographs, but all of the

MAM with Luis

pictures are taken between 1900 and 1910. The most fascinating component is the juxtaposition of pictures taken on picnics, with ladies in long dresses and men in stiff collars and tight-coated suits, with contrasting rustic photographs of a log cabin in the Rocky Mountains of southern Alberta, as well as snapshots of a Yale Commencement placed with another of three men in a CPR boxcar moving camp. Although the events at Yale and those in the boxcar are separated by eight years in time, they are shuffled together in the album in a way that demonstrates the two poles of Adele's life taking shape. She was a city-bred young lady, educated, and acquainted with well-bred, Yale- and Cornell-educated young men. She was accustomed to comfort and security. Beside the photos of city boys with their college letters on their chests are pictures of a stubble-faced, work-booted, adventurer wearing gauntlets and a battered hat, who had already been to Panama and back and had now gone west.

The album makes the choice before her as immediate as it must have been in her own mind, even though the process lasted a decade or more. If she had not been confident in herself, she would not have continued as a spinster to the age of thirty-three. By the time she went north after graduation in 1902, she may well have met Craig Pierce (the adventurer-to-be), who was an eighteen-year-old private-school student in Pittsburgh with two years to go before his graduation. She either knew him then or met him within a very few years when she and her mother returned to live near family in Kittanning, which is very near his home territory of McKeesport. He always said it took him ten years to convince her to marry him – so they knew each other by 1905 at the latest.

The anxieties of maternal and child mortality, which were such a tangible reality in the late nineteenth century, surrounded Adele's own birth especially because the family had intimate experience with the death of babies. Three of the children born in her Uncle Thomas's house died in the few years around Mac and Dellie's births. When Adele was having her babies, thirty-five years later, these same fears were expressed in letters sent and received. After her first child's birth, messages arrived from friends and family who were "so relieved and delighted when it was all over dear,"[22] "so glad the strain is over,"[23] and "so glad it's over and you are all right."[24] Adele wrote to her sister-in-law Pearl Pierce that she "[didn't] believe in getting things like the crib, carriage Etc before hand – Too often the first baby doesn't stay in the world very long."[25] Later, when her baby Laura was four months old, Adele wrote to Pearl again that she "wouldn't leave her for long at a time for anything as the baby of friends of mine turned on his face and was smothered last month and he was just a little older than Laura."[26]

These six letters to Pearl (see appendix B) are generous with information about prenatal nutrition, breast care, and the experience of labour and delivery. Pearl was pregnant with her first child, due a few months after Adele's, and the letters are filled with that enthusiastic willingness to inform the uninitiated that only the suddenly and fully wise can demonstrate. Adele recommends a serial called "Diary of an Expectant Mother" appearing in the *Pictorial Review* starting in January 1917 and encourages Pearl to "write and tell me all your feelings"[27] and to ask "anything in the world"[28] because she herself "would have been glad to have had any one to ask who had recent experience."[29]

Adele reported that her morning sickness lasted only for the first trimester,[30] and for her last trimester she became a devotee of "Tokology," the science of parturition and obstetrics, which at the time advocated a dietary system she believed to be "the right dope" and which she subsequently adhered to "pretty conscientiously – ate hardly any [red] meat and just scads of fruit [. . .] instead of eating solids I filled up on fruit – ate apples by the ton."[31] The object seems to have been as much to keep the baby's birth weight down as it was designed for maternal nutrition. Later in the same letter, Adele noted that "it certainly paid me to take care of myself though. The other women [in the hospital] had eaten unwisely and had great big babies, two were still born [*sic*] because they were so big."[32] There was always that fear of infant mortality.

But also present is Adele's own body consciousness. In one of the letters to Pearl, she confides that:

> The hardest part to me has been looking so sloppy. You know you will never be the same shape again and I am so big and fat. Simply can't wear a thing I ever had before and I never had any breasts to speak of – now they are large and I weigh 30 pounds more than when we were married. Of course, I am wonderfully well – but 168 is some weight![33]

The postpartum realities of shape combine with the metabolic slowdown consistent with her mid-thirties age and reflect with an unpleasant suddenness back to her wedding-day body of only one year earlier. One day she is a bride, and in less than a year she has the loose-muscled jelly belly and ample leaky breasts of a recently delivered nursing mother. Possibly, she also feared her adored husband's reaction to her altered, and perhaps permanently changed, appearance; that he might physically reject her in her sloppy condition is not an unlikely concern for her to experience, especially since he had not seen her for several months including the entire time she was visibly pregnant. Photographs of Adele with her baby, however, show a beaming mother as genuinely engrossed

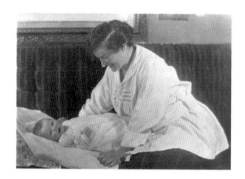

MAM with her first baby

in her accomplishment as her letters suggest. She repeatedly remarks on "the most enthralling subject in the world – babies,"[34] that her Laura "is the prettiest baby I ever saw,"[35] and that baby's care is "the most important"[36] of her duties.

Adele's graduation portrait, taken when she was twenty, shows retrospectively the pre-sloppy body. Her self-awareness and self-presentation exemplify the turn-of-the-twentieth-century woman:

> the "Big American Girl" [. . .] determinedly self-assured, part college girl, part fashionable beauty, [. . .] [with] her pompadoured head [she is] followed everywhere by male admirers. This new American girl was not just exceptionally pretty, she could look you in the eye, had a firm handshake, and strode from the nineteenth century into the twentieth century emancipated, confident and chic."[37]

Her surviving letters make clear a vigorous love for her husband. As was the custom, she travelled home to her mother for her "confinements" when she could, but she "[wrote] to my beau every day"[38] and "almost broke my heart wanting Craig after the baby came [. . .] and cried every day just wanting him so. But now I am strong again and he is coming soon so you can imagine I am wild with joy. He is pret-

MAM's graduation portrait

ty crazy, too."[39] To connect her returning strength in the same sentence with his imminent arrival provides a physical quality to their mutual excitement. To be strong again means to be recovered from childbirth, to have stopped bleeding, to be free to have sex again. She was "too flustered to do anything as the time drew nearer for my Craig"[40] and "got fairly silly with excitement by the time he landed."[41] In fact, she was so agitated that her breast milk failed for the day when he arrived. Wonderfully, she freely declares that she is "more than a little looney about him. Really I think it is almost suffering to care so much – I want him with me every minute."[42] Their youngest daughter remembered that every letter or domestic note her father ever wrote to her mother began simply, "Dearest."

Ten years after the wedding, Adele was forty-three-years old, had moved from Buffalo, New York to an Alberta farm, and had four children between September 1916 and October 1921. The picture below is taken during summer on the prairie – she is not protecting herself from a cold wind. This image and the 1902 graduation portrait shown together might be captioned comically: "Do you think she liked city life or country life better?" Having had no opportunity to control her "sloppy"

MAM in farmyard

body, because she openly desired her husband, who clearly proved her fears of rejection groundless, and was coincidentally an extremely fertile chick, she appears rather less confident about her physical self. She had written confidently, and obviously mistakenly, to her sister-in-law that she had "some good dope to prevent [conception] if you care to know something harmless and very simple."[43] Harmless and simple it may have been, whatever it was, but effective contraception it clearly was not.

By comparison with the vast majority of prairie farmwomen, Adele had so many advantages as to be a woman of leisure. She was never without help in the house; always, there was at least one hired girl throughout her married life, plus a cook on the farm. Although she did do the cooking for her own family always, she did not have to cook for the field hands, and she never had to be a field hand herself. In a community of women who did every single household task from cooking to washing to preserving on their own, plus had to add their labour to that of the men during harvest or tend to the livestock chores, she was by comparison an extraordinarily privileged and pampered woman.

Although Craig provided for her every comfort possible (including winter quarters in the city and frequent journeys home to her mother) and eased her isolation and work so far as he could, she was still an educated Eastern woman thrust into surroundings which were the antithesis

MAM's home on Richmond Avenue in Buffalo

MAM's home on Hurst Avenue in Chautauqua

MAM in furs

of everything that was familiar. From the long-established neighbourhoods of Richmond and Hurst Avenues (where she was born to wear furs), she moved into:

a house such as this was and still is – I can't describe it for you never lived this way and can't imagine it – no water in the house, every drop has to be carried from the wind mill and all to be emptied again, coal fires, coal to carry and ashes to empty, oil lamps, all such things and worst of all the outside toilet away off from the house, almost an impossibility in bad weather [...] The walls were so awful I could not live with them so we have been doing them [...] – but ever so many places the plaster is off & of course they will all have to be done over. The roof leaks & the newly painted walls & ceilings are getting streaked.[44]

She was optimistic, however, and went on to describe plans for improving the house, about getting the lumber hauled, and hiring a car-

MAM's house on the farm in Alberta

45

penter and plasterers for the top floor to have "some more windows cut, partitions, etc."[45] The "bright little spot with two windows [which] will be Craig's office"[46] is a tiny room I remember well from my childhood. It was located on the main floor of the house, in the northwest corner off the living room, and still contained his massive oak roll-top desk. I remember playing school there, beating my dolls with a ruler for being stupid. I wish I knew how Adele dealt with her frustrations and her intellectual needs. By all accounts, it was a completely non-violent household – except for later years when the girls predictably developed territorial issues of their own.

The children were supposed to be born back East with "Mamma," but her second daughter, Hetty, was born in Canada as a result of travel restrictions imposed during the influenza epidemic of 1918. Adele was such an American chauvinist that it was extremely important to her that her children be born in the United States. She was outraged when Hetty eventually opted for Canadian citizenship by voting in an election. How anyone could forfeit American citizenship was beyond her comprehension. One of my very few memories of her is crossing the Canada/U. S. border and hearing her elaborate inhalation as she exhorted us, "Oh children, smell that air!" My sister remembers watching Grandma and her eldest daughter, our Aunt Laura, leap to their feet at the start of a televised baseball game and place their hands over their hearts for "The Star-Spangled Banner."

Laura was born in a hospital but the others were born at home: Hetty in Calgary because of the flu; Lucy in Richmond, Virginia at Uncle Arthur's because of the winter cold; and Mary in the cool of the Chautauqua summer house because of the autumn heat. When he had to remain behind because of harvest and other farm obligations, Craig travelled East later to help bring Adele home, a trip that became more complicated with each birth. On the return trip after Laura was born, they found themselves snowbound for an extra three days on a train near St. Paul, Minnesota in March 1917.[47] Of course, the babies went with Adele when she went East each time, but help was hired to make the journey with her. Nevertheless, the logistics of being on board a train for at least four days and three nights with diapers (cloth, of course) to manage had to be daunting.

When she was just three-months pregnant with Lucy, in August 1919, Adele made the trip (with three-year-old Laura and eight-month-old Hetty) and Craig joined her in January. In the midst of all these trips, at some point during 1919 or 1920, Adele's dear brother Malcolm was admitted to a state mental institution in Allentown, Pennsylvania. During his time at Yale, around the turn of the century, he had been infected with syphilis, and although he had endured the so-called arsenic cure before his marriage, he was one of the unfortunate ones who "develop tertiary syphilis, which may develop after years to decades of latency."[48] Because of the prolonged period of latency, Mac's wife was uninfected, but when the latency ended, his deterioration was sudden and severe.

It is likely that Adele's early departure for the East in August 1919, during her third pregnancy, was precipitated by this turn in her brother's health. Her brother in an asylum, Craig and Adele left Richmond to return by train (with a three-and-a-half-year-old, a fourteen-month-old, and a six-week-old baby) on March 20, 1920 and arrived in Calgary on the 25th.[49] Not surprisingly, as a result of combined physical and emotional stresses, Adele was not-quite-well when they arrived. Six days later, she "went to Holy Cross Hospital for curetment [known now as a D&C]"[50] and was there until April 5th. Craig and a hired nurse stayed at the Empress Hotel tending to the children.[51]

The day Adele was discharged, Laura was taken to the Isolation Hospital because of measles, and the hired nurse went with her. Three days later, Hetty too was admitted with measles; they remained there until April 17th.[52] Undoubtedly, Adele did not visit the older girls in the Isolation Hospital, out of concern for her own health and the baby's. Laura and Hetty were very little girls, only three-and-a-half-years and sixteen-months old, sick and frightened by the separation which lasted almost two weeks. They would not have seen their mother after she went into the hospital herself and so already would have been distressed when immediately after her return they were taken away themselves. The whole family would have been dis-eased in every way possible. A year earlier, with only two little ones and only head colds to manage in the comfort of her mother's presence, her last remaining letter to Pearl opens with the remark that "so much has happened there is no use in my trying to tell you reasons for not writing."[53] What stories she might have written in May of 1920.

The manifestation of her experiences is evident in August 1921, when Adele was thirty-nine years old and seven-months pregnant with her last child. Just before her departure for Chautauqua on the 27th,[54] she is photographed with her three daughters and two other women. It is likely they have just delivered a meal to the fields, as happened through my childhood and still occurs, in order that there is minimal time lost from harvest. She strategically hides her persistently gestating body inside a heavy coat and behind a stook of wheat sheaves. In October, Craig's last journal entry for 1921 states that he "got wire saying fourth daughter had arrived."[55] The family anecdote is told that he remarked,

MAM behind a wheat stook

"You'd think one of them could have been a boy." How they gained con-traceptive control over their very fruitful union is unknown. But given their undisguised love for each other and their impressive tendency to conceive, it is most likely that they simply had to keep away from each other. Having had her babies so closely together, with little recovery time between, and considering her age, there must have been legitimate con-cern for her physical well-being, and perhaps also for her mental welfare.

When her brother Malcolm's disease reached its natural and inevitable conclusion, Adele was nearby, having made yet another trip East at the end of July 1923.[56] I suspect that she was notified of his wors-ening condition and impending death and returned to be with their mother. He died 23 September 1923 at the age of only forty-three. Adele returned to Canada at the beginning of November.[57] It is impossible to know if she visited Mac during any of these journeys, but I find it hard to believe that she did not. Allentown is not so far from Buffalo where their mother and brother Al lived, from Richmond where their brother Arthur lived and where Adele spent the winter of 1919/20, or from Kittanning where Adele and their mother spent the winter of 1921/22.

He was her favoured brother, but the extraordinary stigma of mad-ness comes together with the extraordinary stigma of venereal disease perhaps to create too powerful a social force to overcome. There is no mention of this specific illness (or of any illness) or even of his death in ACP's journals. Mac's wife's fury at her circumstances of loss and feelings of humiliation resulted in her precipitous departure with their five chil-dren from Pennsylvania to Connecticut immediately following his admission to Allentown. The children (except for the youngest on only one occasion) never saw their father again, did not hear their mother speak his name for twenty years after his death, and do not know what she did with his ashes. Perhaps his sister experienced such a shame and anger response that she too stayed away, but I prefer not to think so.

Soon after Adele's return to the farm, the weight of all these events began to take its toll on her. In March 1924, when her last child, Mary, was two-and-a-half, life-style arrangements began to evolve once more.

Adele was in the Holy Cross Hospital once again, this time for two weeks to undergo an appendectomy.[58] A week after her discharge, she was admitted to the hospital in Drumheller for "gastritis and rest" and remained there for another two weeks.[59] At the end of the first week, she still was not eating. The children were taken to visit her once each.[60] On May 10th, Adele went to a physician in Calgary, accompanied by her husband, and she stayed behind in a hotel while he returned to the farm.[61] She remained at the hotel for two weeks with only one visit from her family.[62] I feel confident in supposing that her brother's death precipitated a rather serious depression that was perhaps complicated by the overall mental strain of her childbearing and rearing.

In August of 1925, again on the orders of her doctor, she spent another week in Calgary at a hotel[63]; two months later, she left with the children and a helper to go East for the winter.[64] The children were nine, seven, six, and four, and the helper was clearly a luxury engaged for Adele's sake, being too unwell to manage their care on her own. After two months, Craig arrived to be with his family and return with them at the end of the following March.[65] At the end of October 1926, Adele and the girls moved into a rented house in Calgary.[66] The three older girls were ten, eight, and seven, and although Kirby School (which the children had attended) was within an accessible distance of the farm, the decision was made to educate the girls in the city. After this, they only summered on the farm. Including the 1916/17 year in Saskatchewan, Adele had been a prairie-farm wife for only nine years – with substantial blocks of time away during that period. She simply was not cut out for it.

Adele continued to summer on the farm for a few years, until the girls could do without her supervision, and then even those compromises were suspended. She rarely even went there afterwards. Hetty remembered her mother telling about the water being frozen in the morning, and of sawing a piece of meat from a frozen hind quarter. [. . .] [And of] the reverse in summer, when the struggle was to keep food from spoiling in the heat. We had a screened cupboard with a gunny sack draped over it. The sacking was kept wet, and the evaporation helped to keep things cool. And there was the water trough for milk and butter.[67]

The farmhouse was first listed in the telephone directory of 1922 – the number was R606 – but it did not have running water or electricity until 1944 "when we got a wind charger."[68] It was heated with coal well into my childhood. There was a coal room in the basement with a window to the outside through which the delivery truck could dump its load. At the time Adele gave up rural life, the house was still almost twenty years from developing any appreciable conveniences at all.

In 1938, when her husband held the prestigious position of President of the Calgary Board of Trade, he hosted a large contingent of business people for a luncheon and tour of the farm.[69] She did not attend. While I find her absence noteworthy, to say nothing of odd, there is no indication that a quarrel of any kind erupted over this episode. Craig's journals merely record the names of neighbour women who prepared and served the lunch; he certainly would have recorded her presence if she had been there. It would appear that this is a prime example of his acceptance and accommodation of her lack of affinity for rural life. Apparently he was able to recognize that her rejection of farm life was not also a rejection of him.

After her return to city life, and with the girls getting older and more independent, she and Craig enjoyed short annual vacations to the mountains or to the Pacific Northwest region alone together. She apparently was no longer willing to forsake a more cosmopolitan life in the city. She enjoyed movies very much, and Craig's journals are full of entries which mention her going to various movie houses in the afternoon, often two or three times a week, and she played a great deal of bridge. (They both did.) Women of her time and privilege for the most part did not seek employment outside the home, but often they participated in various committee and charitable works. Adele, however, did not. She was a member of no committees and joined no organizations other than the Women's Institute while she was living on the farm. Her daughter Mary explained simply that "she wasn't a joiner."

In the Calgary years, ACP's journals record almost daily excursions to go "shopping on 11th" where within a block there were grocery, bakery, butcher, and greengrocer shops. Adele sewed, since four daughters required numerous dresses for numerous occasions, and she read extensively, especially enjoying humour (such as Robert Benchley) and mysteries (nothing too gory, according to Mary). She was remembered by her niece as "vivacious"[70] and by her nephew as a woman with a great sense of humour, always laughing.[71] She was prone to acts of kindness: in May 1919 her farm cook was eight-months pregnant and living in a twelve-by-twelve shack; even with her own house in the condition Adele described to Pearl, she invited Mrs. Edwards to come there to have her baby.[72] Her first son-in-law, Hetty's husband Jack, familiarly referred to her as "Mama Toots."

She held all of her opinions very strongly and was not perhaps the most forgiving of women. I recall travelling through Fernie, British Columbia, where my grandparents had once experienced a winter road accident. As we drove past the sign at the town limits, she prompted us, "Sneer, children, sneer," and fifty years after her death I am still unable to keep my upper lip from curling in derision any time I travel through Fernie. She once asked my cousin and me which of her two miniature sets we would like to have. I chose the Blue Willow tea set, which I still have, and Mary Sue chose the cast-iron stove and pots. Too young to understand that she was making plans for bequests, I innocently thought she had asked out of curiosity.

Epilogue

Rural life was an aberration rather than the norm for MAM. After her exile ended, she returned to the world of furs. I remarked to my sister that in this picture Grandma is not dressed appropriately for the occasion; she replied that, since she had no recollection of anyone ever calling Grandma "an outdoor enthusiast," it is the setting and not the wardrobe that is inappropriate. She said that MAM in hiking boots with a rope slung over her shoulder would look stranger than MAM in a fur coat on a mountainside, not overdressed for a casual and genteel excursion in the mountains.

MAM with ACP in the mountains

CHAPTER THREE

ANDREW CRAIG PIERCE (1884–1955)

THE HILLS OF ELIZABETH TOWNSHIP IN Allegheny County, Pennsylvania look like tightly clustered turtles – terrain that secludes and secures some people, but that crowds and insulates others. Southwestern Pennsylvania is farming country. A haven for people such as the Amish, it was created with more pastoral-farming methods in mind, preferring living beasts over mechanical horsepower. The rolling hills around Pittsburgh and McKeesport are not accessible to farming with massive fuel-burning machinery because the fields are too small and the grades too steep for large and ungainly equipment. It could not be less like the vastness of the prairie land and sky that ACP encountered when he first travelled west in 1907 or into southern Alberta in 1909. The sky in Alberta is so enormous that it frightens some newcomers who are unaccustomed to feeling so exposed, the way rabbits and mice feel when a hawk is in the air. On clear days, which are the rule in Alberta, visibility is reported at nine-hundred-ninety-nine miles. The prairie is not a place for the myopic.

ACP's early life was lived as a Pennsylvania farm boy, the youngest of three sons born to Joseph and Henrietta Pierce, and then as a prep-school boy and as a university student. His father was sixty when Craig was born; Henrietta was thirty-eight. There was a ten-year gap between Craig and his older brothers, William Torrence and Joseph Audley, and Craig's twin brother was stillborn. These boys were the sixth generation of the family to live in the region; these three were also the last of this

ACP as a baby

branch of the family to live in rural Pennsylvania.

Craig's first formal portrait was taken at the Dabbs Studio in Pittsburgh, where "Instantaneous Portraits of Children [was] A Successful Specialty," when he was about two years old. Already, his very direct and intense gaze is evident. It is a look that remained unchanged throughout his photographed life: he consistently looks very hard and very far into the distance. Certainly, his post-education and pre-marriage years demonstrate an energetic eagerness to go places far outside his family's experience and realm. His less adventurous brothers, Will and Audley, remained in Pennsylvania, and became city people. Audley graduated from Lafayette College in Easton, Pennsylvania and then the University of Tennessee law school. Craig is the only one of the boys educated at

Shady Side Academy, an all-male Pittsburgh preparatory school established in 1883 and still operating as an independent coeducational institution. Halfway through his studies there, he was already training as a surveyor at the age of eighteen.

Late in Craig's father's life (or perhaps shortly after his death in 1903), the family moved from the farm and went to live in the house at 5899 Bartlett Street in Pittsburgh. The Bartlett Street house is a large two-storey brick house

ACP surveying in Pennsylvania

with three chimneys, leaded panes in the attic dormer windows, and a paved sidewalk leads up to the roofed veranda that stretches across the front of the house. Although the work involved later in surveying the mountains of Colorado had to be difficult and not for the faint-hearted, Craig's prep-school and university education plus the size of this house on Bartlett Street demonstrate that he was a privileged young man born into the ranks of the working wealthy. His travels were not made out of economic necessity but rather were undertaken at the behest of an internal impetus, out of a desire to go, which persisted throughout his life. He takes shape for me as a man restless in body and mind – not a discontented restlessness but a high-energy intellectual curiosity and physicality that drove him to go and see and do, endlessly interested in developments of all kinds.

Henrietta had moved to 5517 Black Street by the time Craig entered Lehigh University in Bethlehem, Pennsylvania as a civil engineering student in the autumn of 1904 when he was twenty. He completed the first two years of his four-year programme but did not choose to return and complete the degree. In a full-page newspaper article by Grant MacEwan (once mayor of Calgary, Lieutenant-Governor of Alberta, and a much-published Alberta historian) ACP is said to have come to Alberta "In 1909, a year after graduation [. . .] as a member of a survey crew working near Gleichen".[1] His daughters always believed he was a *bona fide* civil engineer, but no one

ACP at 20

knows if he led them to believe that or if they made the assumption themselves, assuming that if he started something, he must have finished it. But according to the archives at Lehigh University and West Virginia University, he did not. After Lehigh, the only subsequent opportunity he had to complete the remaining two years of his degree were the academic years 1907/08 and 1908/09. It is extremely likely that he did not graduate, and if he had, we would see his degree framed on the wall of some family member's home.

Photographs showing him with the football squad (the handsome man at the centre of the back row, fourth from the right) and the Phi Kappa Sigma fraternity (back row, on the far right), at West Virginia University in 1908, suggest he may have studied there. However, the university reports that, while he transferred credit from Lehigh and was admitted to the institution, he never enrolled in classes.

His daughter Mary remembered him telling the story that he was the only person ever pledged to some particular fraternity chapter without ever attending the university. Phi Kappa Sigma at WVU must be the society of which he spoke. After he left there, there is never a time when his years are unaccounted for, at least, not for long enough to complete his studies. The family collection includes many photographs of the Cheat River area near Morgantown and Arthurdale, West Virginia. They show a formal camp setting with large tents, and I am convinced that ACP was engaged in some sort of engineering work there. The Cheat River is not only a very popular wilderness area known for its white water, but it also serves as the water supply for the city of Pittsburgh. Perhaps, he supported his varsity-sports habit by working on the project.

His daughter Mary and his nephew James Moore remembered often hearing stories about "Uncle Craig" being what was called a "tramp athlete."[2] Jim believed that Craig attended Lafayette College because he was certain that Craig had played basketball there; however, Lafayette has no record of him. The facts from West Virginia add credibility to Jim's recollections. Craig appears to have moved from campus to campus in order

ACP's football team

ACP's fraternity brothers

to offer his athletic services wherever he could. Mary said that he had a "bad reputation [. . .] not as a bad scholar [. . .] as a playboy [. . .] good-time guy."[3] She says "he went to a lot of universities" and that he "tried to get into The University of Washington in Seattle,"[4] but the University of Washington has no record of him at all. It is conceivable that he did indeed spend two years in West Virginia; he just never went to class.

Lehigh University required applicants to pass a series of entrance examinations. To qualify for admission to Civil Engineering in the School of Technology, Craig was required to complete successfully seven separate exams: English, American History, Algebra, Geometry, Plane Trigonometry and Logarithms, Elementary Physics, and German. As soon as regulations permitted, ACP was pledged, initiated, and housed by Phi Delta Theta. This was clearly an important affiliation for him because he remained an active Phi Delt for the rest of his life, visiting with fraternity brothers when he could and often finding accommodations even thirty years later at various chapter houses when he travelled for business and political purposes.

Since Greek-letter societies are secret societies, the histories of Phi Delta Theta do not reproduce "the Bond, the basic law of the fraternity."[5] However, the six men who founded the fraternity in 1848 at Miami University in Oxford, Ohio are all described as

> men of good digestion and sound physical constitution, hence little if anything morbid characterized their views [. . .] [their] private lives were without reproach and above suspicion [. . .] [each man was] connected with some church by credible profession of his faith in Christ [. . .] conscientious, God-fearing men [. . .] they were brave men; they were not blusterers, and of course not cowards [. . .] men of decided convictions.[6]

Craig regularly attended church services throughout his life in Calgary at Wesley United Church, accompanied by one or the other of his daughters. Adele almost never went. The Sunday morning routine,

Wesley United Church in Calgary

according to both Hetty and Mary, was for ACP to call up the stairs: "some of you fellas better get up and come to church with me."

When he was on the farm, services were conducted by community men at nearby Kirby School, and ACP regularly took his turn with the sermon. His church involvement helps explain the appeal of his chosen fraternity, because when it was founded, the new Phi Delta Theta brotherhood set itself apart from other societies on the basis that other groups

> had reference to talent, to the head alone; ours includes both the head and the heart as alike essential. It is not the influence of the open outlaw, the depraved debauchee or the avowed infidel that is so injurious to society; it is the deep undercurrent of immorality and infidelity in literature, emanating from sources unsuspected and for that reason the more dangerous.[7]

When Craig entered the fraternity, he was one of fifteen men[8] in the eighteen-year-old Pennsylvania Eta chapter, so called because it was the seventh Pennsylvania chapter of the fraternity.[9] If the woman he married "was not a joiner," he certainly was. Over the years, he had so many committees and organizations in which he actively and regularly participated, their lives would have been in a state of chaos if Adele had obligated herself outside the home even to a fraction of the work he did. Phi Delta Theta is his first known membership, but his obituary[10] lists him as also

a member of McKeesport Lodge No. 641, AF and AM [Ancient Free and Accepted Masons]; McKeesport Chapter No. 282, RAM [Royal Arch Masons]; McKeesport Commandery No. 86 [Knights Templar, also Masonic]; Tourgas [sic] Lodge of Perfection [Gourgas Lodge, also Masonic], Pittsburgh, Penn.; Al Azhar Shrine Temple, Calgary; Syria Temple [also Shrine], Pittsburgh; Rose Croix Pennsylvania Consistory [also Masonic], Pittsburgh, and the Ranchmen's Club [a Calgary business-men's club].

The list omits his membership in the Benevolent and Protective Order of Elks (B.P.O.E.), into which he was initiated 26 February 1907, and the Renfrew Club, a Calgary club where he played bridge, read, and where Board of Trade meetings were held.

Altogether, he held membership in five Masonic Lodges, two Shrine Temples, one Elks Lodge, and two Greek-letter fraternities (initiated a Phi Delt, and "once a Phi Delt always a Phi Delt" but also pledged as an honorary Phi Kappa Sigma). However, all of his Masonic affiliations, his Elks membership, the Syria Shrine, and both fraternities are alliances that he formed while living in Pennsylvania as a young man before his permanent departure in 1907 when he was twenty-three. While he maintained his connections with these various orders sufficiently for them to warrant itemization in his obituary, and his journals regularly mention Shrine functions and contain some oblique mentions of Masonic functions, he apparently did not feel a life-long need to align himself with more and more lodge organizations. These alliances were superseded and their function served in later years by more public groups in the form of committees and councils, both agricultural and political. The primary conclusion to be drawn from his fraternal memberships is that he was deeply committed to the idea and the practice of brother-hood.

During his sophomore year at Lehigh, "the fundamental subjects of Mathematics, Physics, and English [were] completed, and the technical work of civil engineering [was] begun."[11] This second year of study quite literally set his career in motion. This is the year in which he learned the various skills he used as his profession during the widespread travels which began soon after. According to Lehigh's calendar, second-year students have a programme in which:

> The theory of Land Surveying is begun and is accompanied by field work and map drawing [. . .] The work in Topographic Surveying is done in the four weeks following the end of the Sophomore year. In Railroad Surveying both preliminary and final locations of a line are made, and plans, profiles, and estimates of cost are prepared. In Geodetic Surveying triangulations of a high degree of precision are executed, as also determinations of azimuth, and adjustments of the results are made by standard methods [. . .] Under the head of Construction are grouped the topics of masonry, foundations, roads and pavements, cements and mortars, walls, dams, arches, tunnels, and details of structures.[12]

All of this academic and practical preparation brought ACP to the autumn of 1906 and the end of his formal education.

At least some of the eight-month period back in Pittsburgh after leaving Bethlehem had to be spent planning his forthcoming major expedition, which I believe was undertaken probably as a surveyor in the employ of a railroad company. His second-year studies certainly included useful preparation for work on railways. This speculation is also based on verbal information from his daughter Hetty (my mother) and others that he did at some time work as a surveyor. In addition, there are many photographs from a four-month trip between April and August in 1907, and those which span the next several years are variously inscribed by

ACP in a boxcar

ACP as taken in CPR engineer camps around Brooks, Alberta and at the Carbon Hill Coal Company cabin in the Rocky Mountains west of Pincher Creek, Alberta. In this photograph, he is shown (at centre) living in a CP boxcar in July 1910. Canadian Pacific kept no employee records at the time, and surveyors were contract workers rather than CP employees anyway, so the photographs are the only proof there is.

When he left New York on April 27, 1907, bound for Colon, the U.S. Army Corps of Engineers was taking control over construction of the Panama Canal. The project had been undertaken by France and the work done by civilian engineers before the American military intervention. Shortly after his travels began, he acquired a new camera and subsequently recorded his journeys visually. He may have been a journal keeper all through that time, but, if he was, those books are lost. His volume for 1919 does mention a 1918 book, so perhaps he was a life-long diarist; unfortunately, the books did not survive until Craig began to lead a less itinerant life. Unless they are in an archive somewhere, perhaps in Pittsburgh. What written evidence there is for his travels of 1907 exists on the outside of a stationery box and on the backs of photographs. Happily, his penchant for detail, recording, and measuring, which is so evident in the journals, made him unable to resist the need to calculate how far he had travelled and how long it had taken him to do it.

Before the discovery of the calculations on the box, it was merely family lore which maintained that he had been to Panama. That he worked on the Canal, at least for the Isthmian Canal Commission, is apocryphal – correspondence with the U.S. Army Corps of Engineers, U.S. Army Center of Military History, U.S. Army Engineer Centre, and Civilian Records at the National Archives and Records Administration uncovered no military or civilian connection with the engineers or any branch of the armed services at any time or in any place for ACP. However, there was a Panama Railroad Company, and I think it very possible that it is the missing connection. He certainly did not go to Panama as a tourist, not in 1907. He continued from there to Colorado, where he spent seven weeks in various locations around Colorado Springs and Denver, and by the autumn was camped, and also apparently at work, by the Cheat River in West Virginia. Railroads provided continuity to his travels, which I am confident were undertaken in the employ of a rail or mine company or a combination of the two. Written in pencil on the lid of the stationery box are some of the dates and places, which help to chart his journey. The bottom of the Highland Linen Bond box reveals his mileage (see following page for a transcription).

Although the two-hundred miles of travel in Panama seems short, the isthmus is only fifty miles across, from deep water to deep water. Because ACP was there only for five or six days, he managed an average of thirty-five or forty miles per day – a fairly rigorous pace given conditions at the time. He bought and preserved several large picture-postcard images, which he dated on the back and glued into an album to record the sights there. He must have purchased his replacement camera when he arrived for a two-day stopover in Kingston, Jamaica on May 16th. The photographs taken then are not captioned except for street location but are images of the rubble left by the earthquake of January 14th, 1907.

ACP's engineering background, and in particular the training in structural and geological matters, no doubt caused him to be fascinated

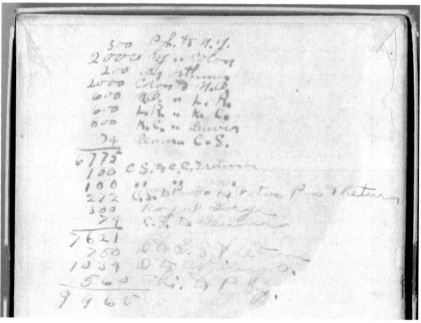

ACP's stationery box

Apr.	27	N.Y. Lv.
May	5	Colon Arr
"	11	Colon Lv
"	16	Kingston Ar
"	18	" Lv.
"	22	N.O.[New Orleans]
"	23–29	Lr [?]
"	29 June 12	
June	12 –	Colo Springs

500	Pgh. to N.Y.[Pittsburgh New York]
2000	N.Y. " Colon[Colon, Panama]
200	On Isthmus
2000	Colon to N.O.[New Orleans]
600	N.O. " L.R.[Little Rock]
600	L.R. " K.C.[Kansas City]
800	K.C. " Denver
74	Denver " C.S.[Colorado Springs]
6775	
100	C.S. to C.C. & return [Cripple Creek, CO]
100	" " "
272	C.S. to Pueblo La Vitas [?] Pass & Return
300	Royal Gorge
74	C.S. to Denver
7621	
750	D. to G.S & return [Glenwood Springs CO]
1034	D. to Chicago.
560	Chi. to Pbg.
9965	

Transcription of ACP's mileage record

with the effects of a magnitude 6.5 earthquake on an urban centre. Perhaps he even went to Jamaica expressly for the purpose of observation and not merely to take a connecting ship to New Orleans for the next leg of his journey. Taken four months after the fact, the photographs show a devastated city. The Significant Earthquakes Database indicates that one thousand people died and thirty-million dollars' damage was done. After his stop in Jamaica, ACP spent his twenty-third birthday on a boat between Kingston and New Orleans.

He spent the next several years roaming, but not aimlessly. Pieced together from the little he recorded on the backs of photographs is an itinerary that took him all over the contiguous United States and into Canada. Aside from the outline pencilled on the stationery box, he also visited Fort Leavenworth, Kansas before heading into Colorado; the only surviving photographs of that outing are of cavalry exercises. Next are pictures taken hiking up the rail bed on Pike's Peak, others at Colorado Springs where he stayed at a boarding house on North Tejon Street, and those from Cripple Creek, Glenwood Springs, Williams Cañon, and Royal Gorge. There are also pictures of social outings and townspeople, but none of these are captioned. One photograph of a well-dressed woman wearing a veiled hat and holding a box camera in her lap is cryptically identified only as "B. B." MAM had entertained other romantic possibilities, such as Luis, during her single years and it would be odd if ACP had not also.

His work in Colorado was interrupted when he spent twelve days in Denver Mercy Hospital after his appendix was removed. From his bed, he photographed the nurse and orderly and later the surgeon in the hallway and a lounge area. He had someone else photograph him on the front steps of the hospital when he was discharged on 1 August 1907. He returned to Pittsburgh via Chicago after his release from the hospital and then spent several months at least, and as much as two years, in West Virginia. By the summer of 1909, Craig was on the move again and working on the Ness ranch at Pendleton, Oregon, but no one knows how he came to know the owner and get the job. The selection of photographs taken during his time there includes several large mule teams complete with whip-wielding mule skinners and the working men and women on the ranch (both Caucasian and Aboriginal).

These photographs were taken not only to record for himself the new world in which he lived, but also to show those who remained Easterners the markedly changed life he had chosen. After the 1909 harvest was finished, Craig left for southern Alberta and was in and around Brooks in a CPR engineer camp during November and December. In March 1910, he was back in Colorado Springs, Colorado, but for April and May he returned to Pendleton, presumably for spring seeding and other field work. He was there again in September–October of that year, but that was the last of his employment with the Ness family. He had been in Alberta for the summer of 1910 and returned there via Seattle and Victoria after the Oregon harvest.

While he was a Ness hand, he had an unusual portrait taken by the Wheeler Studio in Pendleton. The handwritten inscription on the back of the original is in MAM's handwriting and reads "Craig – Wheat ranching in Oregon August 1909." The picture is a favourite for everyone in the family; my mother copied it and the graduation portrait of her mother as a framed gift set for her four children. ACP is twenty-five in this picture, unshaven, and looking very comfortable and confident in his life as a hard-working man. He clearly is not outside his element without bulky ties

ACP ranching in Oregon

and jaw-scraping collars. He was less transient in 1911, working around Bassano and Crowfoot in southern Alberta and was employed on the Van Orsdale farm during this time, becoming life-long friends with the family. He wintered away from the harshness of the prairies even then, as well as in the early years of his marriage: January 1912 found him at the Grand Canyon in Arizona and Mojave, California; January 1913 yielded pictures of New Orleans, Louisiana and El Paso, Texas; and in 1914 he visited Charleston, South Carolina. These far-reaching excursions no doubt framed regular trips home to Pennsylvania, where his mother and brothers still lived, and of course to New York State to see MAM.

During 1911 or 1912, Craig bought his own farming equipment, even though he owned no land, and began contract farming in southern Alberta. It was in 1912 that he bought his first Holt Caterpillar track-type tractor, beginning an agricultural love affair that never ended. In a glossy, sixteen-page Holt advertising publication dating from the late 1930s, ACP's Diesel D4 (purchased in 1936) is featured at work on the cover, and in a full-page series of quotations, he outlines his history with the machinery.

> My first one was a front-wheel type 'Sixty' built during the winter of 1911–12. I have done a considerable part of my farm work with one of them each and every year since, beginning with 1912. In 1919 I purchased a front-wheel type 'Seventy-Five' to use in plowing our heavy gumbo soil [...] In 1928, I purchased one of the smallest, known as the '2-ton,' for pulling a rod-weeder, cultivators and hauling [...] I expected great things of the Diesel D4, purchased in April (1936), [...] to cut operating costs. [...] Everyone of us who has driven the Diesel D4 is unanimous in saying it is the most satisfactory tractor ever handled. 'Caterpillar' track-type Tractors have had a lot to do with my making a go of wheat farming.[13]

The *SRM News* used a photograph, taken in May 1937, of the Sixty, 2-ton, and D4 in our farmyard to underscore a request from Calgary's

Glenbow Foundation for "as much information as possible on the earliest uses of Caterpillar-built tractors" in order to "complete the early history of the Province of Alberta."[14]

After two years of contract work in Alberta (1912–13), ACP went to Saskatchewan where he spent four years (1914–17). At least three of these years, and probably all four, were spent at Leipzig (approximately one hundred miles west of Saskatoon) managing a seed farm, which was owned by the F. A. Owen Publishing Company in Chicago. Certainly he was there before his marriage. During the spring of 1915, just four months before their wedding, he sent MAM a postcard made from a photograph of his Cat at work, with "A. C. Pierce" stencilled on the canopy. He was on his way to a business meeting, he wrote, but "Wish I were taking the train for Chau." and signed it simply "C."

He had spent seven years farming in the west by this time, a completely different prospect from farming in Pennsylvania, and had proceeded through the ranks as though through a corporation: from seasonal hired hand, to contract work with his own machinery, to farm management, becoming less and less transient in direct proportion to his progress through the ranks. He did not, however, entirely privilege the practical over the theoretical. Several texts from his formal education maintained a place on his shelves and are on my shelves now. One is the *Complete Secondary Algebra* he used during his senior year at Shady Side Academy in 1904; two are Loney's 1900 *Elements of Statics* and 1901 *Elements of Dynamics* from his time at Lehigh during 1904–06; two are Le Conte's 1908 edition of *Elements of Geology* and the 1909 Campbell's *Soil Culture Manual*.

The geology text is compatible with engineering study, but the soil-culture text and Henry's *Feeds and Feeding*, which was added to his library after 1914 in Calgary, are more specifically agricultural manuals and contain scientific studies, observations, and evaluations of soil types and crop and stock development. The Campbell text is subtitled "A Complete Guide to Scientific Agriculture as Adapted to the Semi-Arid Regions," which inland Oregon and the prairies certainly were and are.

Thus, the book had obvious value for ACP as he accustomed himself to the requirements and considerations of farming in a new place. Various feeds and feeding ratios are charted in the Henry "Hand-Book for the Student and Stockman" to demonstrate the success and failure of variant animal-husbanding methods. ACP did not just practise agriculture; he studied it. He was nothing if not methodical. Mary, his youngest daughter, remembered that it took great patience to have ACP explain anything because he was so meticulous in his instructions: "now here's a nut and you put it on top of the screw and you turn it."[15] All of this preparation was completed before he ever bought so much as an acre of land for himself, and his self-imposed apprenticeship lasted ten years.

His courtship lasted those same ten years, a duration imposed by MAM – their daughters Hetty and Mary both suggested that he was "a rounder" and she would not marry him until he settled down. After he held a job and a fixed address for two years, she relented, and they were married in Buffalo, New York on December 9th, 1915. If she compromised for him by giving up her life of ease in the East, he also compromised for her by giving up his life of adventuresome travel that undoubtedly would have taken him all over the world if his itchy feet had been left to their own devices. Her demand and need for stability and his for freedom found a place to be together in the open and uncrowded spaces of the Canadian prairie where opportunities existed to satisfy both their ambitions. There does not seem to be a single voice of doubt that theirs was a love match, but it was a match that faced no greater problem than geography – she was Eastern, urban, and American by conviction to the end of her life – and it was a substantial problem that was never wholly resolved for either of them because of the constant necessity for renegotiation and sacrifice by each in the interests of the other.

Craig and Adele's wedding trip was a journey to Florida by ship from New York to Tampa, staying in St. Petersburg and Key West, and cruising to Pasa Grille Island. They saw and photographed porpoises from the ship's deck, giant sea turtles from the dock, palm trees outside their hotel, and pelicans in flight during their holiday which stretched into January.

By the time the honeymoon ended, Adele was pregnant, and when the time came for Craig to return to Saskatchewan for seeding in the spring of 1916, he went alone. Others who worked on the seed farm lived in soddies (small dwellings made of stacked slabs of prairie sod), some with families, but during 1916 a brand new two-storey, hip-roofed house was built, and it is there that Craig took Adele and their baby daughter Laura in the spring of 1917. They likely stayed only until after harvest and then wintered in New York and Pennsylvania with family. They moved to a rented home in Calgary early enough the following year to be listed in *Henderson's (1918) Calgary Directory* and Henrietta Torrence, their second daughter and my mother, was born in December. In 1918, Craig purchased the farm at Drumheller where he solidified his reputation as an agriculturist, as "a wheat grower and power farmer."[16]

The original two-and-a-half-section (two-and-a-half square miles) farm was largely unbroken land when he bought it from William

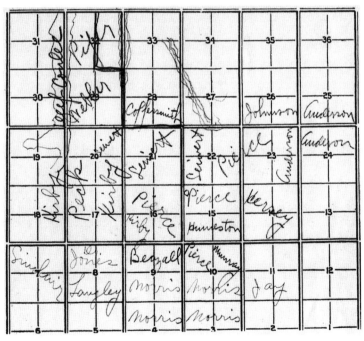

ACP's hand-lettered township map

Dougan, one of many Iowans with land in the region, for $65 an acre. The total purchase price came to $104 000, an enormous amount of money in 1918, but subsequently ACP and Dougan renogotiated a more realistic price of $40 per acre, a total price reduction of $40 000. The home quarter is the NW ¼ 15 T28 R21 W4. The grid system of land measurement used on the prairies is very precise but does require some initial decoding. Reading from right to left, the description becomes more specific until it pinpoints the site on which the rural residence is built. W4 means west of the fourth meridian – not the prime meridian that runs through Greenwich, but the one which serves as the Alberta-Saskatchewan border. The R stands for Range; a range is a township (or six sections) wide and extends to the northern and southern limits of the grid.

The higher the range number, the farther west from the meridian – in this case the provincial boundary – the land is. The T stands for Township, which is a block of thirty-six sections arranged six high and six wide; township numbers are higher the farther north they are. A section is one square mile. The tricky part of the township system is that the south (bottom) six sections are numbered east to west (1–6), then the next six (moving north) are numbered west to east (7–12), snaking back and forth so that the eastern edge of a township consists of the six sections numbered, from south to north: one, twelve, thirteen, twenty-four, twenty-five, and thirty-six. Each section consists of six hundred and forty acres and is divided into four quarters, a quarter-section being the smallest saleable unit of prairie farmland, and the quarters are designated by their compass-point location: NW, NE, SW, and SE. ACP's handwritten record of township twenty-eight lists the neighbourhood as it existed the year he bought the farm. The squiggly lines in sections twenty-seven and thirty-three indicate the Horseshoe Canyon.

According to the 1956 municipal map, Pierce holdings amounted to four-and-a-quarter sections, which is the largest acreage the farm reached. The total amount of land ACP farmed at one time was four thousand acres, but the additional two sections are accounted for by the contract work done for corporate owners. The land location NW ¼ 15 T28 R21 W4 means that the buildings on our farm are located in the northwest quarter of section fifteen of township twenty-eight in range twenty-one west of the fourth meridian. Various fields on our farm are known by their section number. If someone is working "down on 10" it means the work is being done about a mile straight south of the house. Urban people have street addresses; rural people have land descriptions. Roads and highways most often follow these grid lines, which explains why prairie highways are so straight and seem to go on forever.

The highway which runs past the farmyard today was never paved during ACP's years there. What road there was, he graded and maintained using the Cats in an arrangement with the municipality. Banks, grain traders, and insurance companies, whose clients defaulted, foreclosed on mortgages and promissory notes, thus becoming landowners. ACP's journals refer to the "Bank half [section]" or the "M'f'g Life half

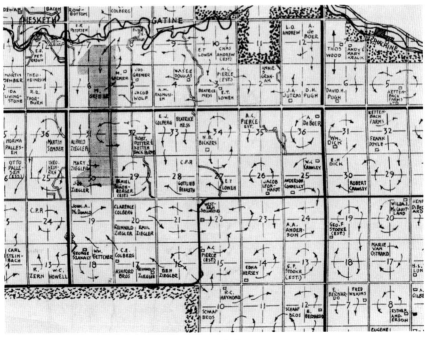

ACP's municipal district map

[section]"; as the land was resold to farmers, the acreage ACP worked would decrease. Farming such a sizeable place required close attention, endless work hours, much equipment, men, and, in the early days, horses. Harvest involved a few more steps when the ratio of men to equipment was greater than one-to-one, as it is now.

In 1924, a ripe crop was put through a six-step process before it was taken to the bin for storage: the standing crop was cut, then horse-drawn binders bundled the grain, men stooked the bundles, and the stooks were later pitched into a horse-drawn rack and taken to the thresher to be threshed – the wheat separated from the chaff. On one very productive day of harvesting in 1924, one thousand eight hundred and fifty bushels were threshed by a dozen men, some horses, and a variety of machinery and equipment. Sixty-years later, three men with two combines and a truck could harvest and bin eight-thousand bushels in a single day. There is no longer any bundling, stooking, or pitching; the six steps are now three. The combine goes to the swath instead of the other way around, and the teams of horses and transient threshing crews (the stookers and pitchers) are long gone.

Mechanical innovations were always welcome in ACP's world. He was fascinated and excited by technology, as his journals and photographs can attest. He had a radio well before his neighbours and once even took his set to Kirby School, where community functions were held, for a dance. Jim Moore, who travelled from Connecticut to spend the summer of 1928 working for his Uncle Craig, remembered ACP using the radio to awaken the hands every morning, and specifically remembers hearing Australian dance music.[17] There is a newspaper clipping which confirms his memory and describes the radio as "a costly mercury super-ten, one of Canadian make."[18] ACP's journals frequently mention the far-off places his short-wave radio picked up, including Mexico City, Spain, and Italy. Because of his fascination with equipment, he photographed machines – preferably machines at work, starting with his pictures of a very flimsy-looking bi-plane taken in Spokane in 1910. The use of workhorses was phased out earlier on the Pierce Farm than on neighbouring land. His photographic collection visually documents the mechanization of agriculture, and his journals record his investigations into new developments.

All of the equipment maintenance was done on the farm in the shop, either by ACP and Crawley (his right-hand man in the early years) or Smyth (who was "an employee on the farm for 22 years"[19] and who had taught Mechanics at the Provincial Institute of Technology). Some of the equipment was even made on the farm, including the transitional method of the harvesting barge which, as the name implies, is a large combination apparatus which cuts the crop, loads it into a holding tank where a worker continuously tramps it down, and periodically unloads great stacks of compacted grain at intervals around the field, ready for threshing. ACP recorded in his journal that he had been to observe a barge demonstration by Costello, a Calgary implement dealer, and was impressed with its potential, but rather than purchase one, he and the men built one, which was used experimentally during harvest 1935.

His agricultural innovations were not solely technological but also environmental. When he bought the place, there was not a tree on it. But, he "came into prominence by his successful development of windbreaks, taking advantage of the Dominion Government's tree planting policy for his seedlings."[20] The tree planting started in 1924, and a dozen years after ACP's death in 1955, newspaper columnist John Schmidt describes as "electrifying" the sight of "at least 110,000 trees growing."[21] A 1976 *Reader's Digest* article says the "21 miles of caragana and four miles of poplar and elm [. . .] turn [ACP's] farm into a regional showplace."[22] Schmidt describes the "miles of trees [. . .] planted in an east–west direction to break the force of the prevailing winds which [. . .] were periodically lifting tons and tons of the dark brown soil from this and many other Prairie farms" as an "arboreal oasis,"[23] which they are to this day. The trees were acquired from the federal government's permanent nursery (established in 1903) at Indian Head, Saskatchewan.

It was not until a decade after ACP started planting trees that Parliament passed the Prairie Farm Rehabilitation Act of 1935 in response to the fact that "the topsoil on 18 million acres, a fourth of all the arable land in Canada, was literally blown away."[24] The destructive winds and drought began as early as May 1926, when ACP recorded a "dust storm in P.M. and all night – very bad."[25] A week later it was "very windy all day – worst dust storm ever at 6:30 – so dark had lamps lighted. House full of dirt."[26] In April of 1933, however, he was able to write "no soil drifting here."[27] Caragana, which "averages a foot of growth in each of the first five years [and] reaches 25 feet at maturity,"[28] is extraordinarily hardy and kept the Pierce farm topsoil where it belonged during the dry and dirty thirties, which were catastrophic years for prairie farmers. Shelterbelts not only control soil drifting but also result in moisture conservation, which in turn affects crop yield.

The farm occupied all of his labours in the early years, and he was always at work side-by-side with the men. There were no tasks too menial for him (even sewing grain sacks), and his journals record each day who was busy at what chore using which piece of equipment. Once the decision was made that the girls should be schooled in the city (approximately seventy-five miles to the southwest), and the farm was well established and thriving, ACP began to spend more time away from the land – never losing touch by any means – and his attention turned once again to more global things and to work of other kinds. The winter of 1925/26 was the last winter Adele and the girls spent in the East. A city home had to be established if the girls were to be regularly at school, and Laura was ten years old that fall. ACP's mother died in June, and he made a quick trip to Pittsburgh. Hetty, who was seven-and-a-half at the time, remembered her father "crying like a baby when word came that his mother had died." His weakened ties to the East, caused in part by the absence of his mother, and the girls' educational considerations made necessary by their ages, worked together to prepare the way for ACP's developing commitment to Calgary. In 1929, he coached the girls' basketball team at Crescent Heights High School. Then, in 1932, he joined the Calgary Board of Trade, now known as the Calgary Chamber of Commerce.

By 1934, and for a period of four years, he organized and was chairman of the Board's farmers' short course, an annual forum jointly sponsored with the provincial Department of Agriculture for discussion and debate, which was always very well attended by urban and rural people alike for whom agriculture was of vital importance. In 1935, he founded and became chairman of the Board's agriculture bureau, which oversaw the short course, and in 1938, when he was fifty-four, he was elected president of the four-hundred-eighty-six member Board of Trade, the first farmer president of a board of trade in the country. These were significant years for ACP to be positioned as an authoritative voice with access to ears at every level of government, and the electorate as well, and he worked vigorously to use his venue to fullest effect in order to address those issues that threatened everyone during the Depression. Editorial remarks in *The Camrose Canadian* recall

ACP in 1936

> the leadership he gave to Alberta farmers, for he prodded them out of their lethargy in the difficult times and brought them together for discussions of their problems, with the result that his neighbours took a new lease on life, a new interest in their industry and lifted themselves up by their bootstraps, so to speak.[29]

In 1938, John Bracken, then Premier of Manitoba, decided to assemble a standing committee of approximately thirty men who would lobby persistently for the federal government to resolve wheat marketing issues. Bracken announced that ACP was "one of the first men asked, and one of the first to accept, a place on the continuing committee."[30] ACP believed that "the operation of a wheat board, and a fixed price for grain, [were] essential to the national economy,"[31] and in 1939 he went to Ottawa with the Bracken Committee to meet with Prime Minister King and his Cabinet, as well as with other party leaders. The unanimity of the delegation and the thoroughness of their presentation directly resulted in the government's decision not to disband the wheat board as had been intended.

The lines were clearly drawn along party lines and when John Bracken became leader of the federal Progressive Conservatives, ACP continued to work with him and campaign for Conservative candidates, declaring that "a Liberal vote is approving removal of the wheat board [...] but a vote for your Bracken Progressive Conservative candidate is a vote for a party which will keep the wheat board in operation and pay parity prices."[32] He reminded voters, through newspaper articles and radio addresses, that it was the Calgary Conservative Prime Minister R. B. Bennett who had enlisted John I. McFarland (who planned the principles of the Canadian Wheat Board between 1930 and 1935) to oversee stabilization of grain prices, and it was Mackenzie King's Liberals who had given him "shabby treatment" and dismissed him.

His political involvement always had an agricultural focus. The United Farmers of Alberta was also a beneficiary of ACP's determined efforts on behalf of western agriculture, and in 1938 he "participat[ed] in [its] series of radio broadcasts re minimum price for wheat and collection of arrears of taxes, etc. in the drought area."[33] Seemingly tireless, he also was appointed to the Alberta wartime crop production committee and was general chairman for the Southern Alberta area of the Canadian War Services Fund drive to which he gave all his time and undertook to organize all of Southern Alberta outside of Calgary.[34] One aspect of the drive was an arrangement by which farmers could make donations in bushels of wheat.

Although he never became a Canadian citizen, ACP clearly considered himself Canadian in many ways and demonstrated his commitment by aligning himself with Canadians on Canadian issues and by his outspoken and energetic political and agricultural activity. He was fund raising for Canadian soldiers before Pearl Harbor brought the United States into WWII; Canadian concerns were his concerns. I am convinced that had it not been for Adele's explicit dislike of this country, he would have taken citizenship and campaigned for political office of his own, as rumour has it he was encouraged to do. That he did not become a citizen is in fact inconsistent with his life-long practice of formally joining groups of many sorts with which he shared convictions and goals. Exclusion from the polling station, when he exhorted others on the importance of exercising their votes, must have been a frustration for him, one that it was uncharacteristic of him to tolerate when the solution was so simple and so accessible.

In spite of his extremely full public schedule and his regular attendance on the farm, ACP managed to be part of his family's daily life. Because the women in the house did not drive, he devoted a great deal of time to his duties as their chauffeur. The fact that none of the girls or Adele had driver's licences puzzled me until Mary explained that ACP refused to teach them how to drive unless they also agreed to "learn how to change a tire, what is a gasket, and what is a carburetor, [then] you can learn how to drive and you can have a car."[35] The response, according to Mary, was that "we learned to drive from our boyfriends."[36] Just as their mother was delivered to movies and bridge games and then collected when she was done, they had to be dropped off and picked up at all their assorted activities, including school when it was too cold for them walk. In 1934, when the girls were aged from eighteen to thirteen, driving almost became a full-time job. The family enjoyed vacations together each year. As early as 1923 they spent a week during July in the mountains.

He considered the girls' birthday parties important enough to be written into his journals along with functions of a far more public nature.

My mother's fourth birthday is written there. Whether he was at home or out in public, his character remained fundamentally the same: MAM's niece Jane Warner remembered him as "dignified" and softly spoken,[37] and Mary said that "maybe at some time during our lives I heard my dad say 'damn' but I don't recall. He never swore."[38] While I have no memories of my own of my grandfather, I have never heard a single negative word about him. When I was a child still living on the farm, it was quite common for old men who had worked for him even one season to be brought by their grandsons to visit the farm a last time. Mary said "everybody respected him,"[39] and I know that to the end of her life my mother could not speak of him without getting tears in her eyes. When I asked Mary about the leadership of the family, she replied that "he was the boss of the whole house." Even of your mother? "He was the boss of everything."[40]

Epilogue

When I was growing up, this portrait was set just above a small display shelf which held his gavel from the presidency of the Calgary Board of Trade. Together, they held a shrine-like significance in our house. The intensity of his gaze is unchanged from the one already evident in the

Dabbs portrait taken when he was two. The worst things I know about him are that he smoked and that he did not want his daughters to work (because "ladies" did not). But, he did nothing to stop them when they went out and got jobs anyway. ACP was inducted posthumously into the Alberta Farmers' Hall of Fame in 1968, and a medal was given in his honour as the prize for the seed competition that he had established.

ACP late in life

He has always been a larger-than-life character for me, and it is unlikely that anything ever will make much of a change in my perception. I enjoy his diversity immensely, love that he gathered flowers from the yard to decorate the house for my mother's wedding day, love that he listened very regularly to opera broadcasts and the World Series on the radio, love his love for my father whom he "loved like he was his son,"[41] love that he put bootleggers up for the night when their car broke down.[42] Although I am unable to relate to his pleasure in bowling, I forgive him for it because he recorded my birth with the declaration that I was "a perfect specimen with no blemishes."[43]

CHAPTER FOUR

LAURA ALLISON PIERCE (1916–1959)

S HE IS THE MISSING SISTER TO ME – the mystery sister. She is the one of whom I have absolutely no memory – even though I was seven-and-a-half when she died. Mary claimed that Laura could knit Argyle socks in the dark. Hetty remembered that she had pretty breasts, such an intimate memory of a sister. Writing Laura raises more questions than it answers, but what details there are serve at least to create a clear idea of the complicatedness of her life. She was given her maternal grandmother's first and maiden names. Laura was born September 7, 1916, three days short of the cultural nine-month requirement after her parents' wedding. People counted out loud in those days. My grandmother even received a gently teasing letter from a

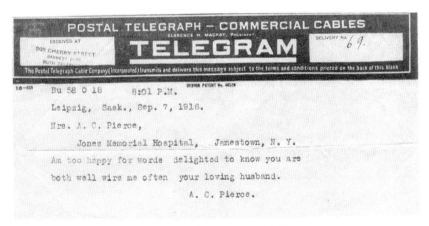

ACP's telegram to MAM

friend remarking on the early arrival: "Not even a full nine months – You lack <u>three days</u>, and I think that's a great joke on Dellie – I'll bet you are grinning yourself."[1] Laura is the only one of the sisters to have a baby book and the only one born in a hospital: Jones Memorial Hospital in Jamestown, New York.

She is the only one of the Pierce children whose likeness was used in an advertisement and the only one with an album of formal baby portraits. She is the only one whose childhood letters survive. All of these things, along with locks of hair, meticulous records of her growth during her first year, and infant-feeding guidelines are tucked in the pages throughout her baby book. According to that book, she arrived at one o'clock in the morning on a Thursday, and she weighed seven pounds and remained in the hospital for two-and-a-half weeks, until September 25th, before she rode home in a taxi twenty miles to her Grandma Moore's house in Chautauqua. She was born first, and she died first. There are three pivotal events in her history that are of such import they become the shaping moments for the family as a whole. All three of these incidents concern her body, and all three occurred before she reached the age of fifteen.

When Laura was almost five years old, her father's 1921 journal tells us, a hired worker on the family farm molested her. ACP wrote that he fired the man "for handling Laura."[2] Martin Crownberg had worked on the farm for six weeks. There can be no real doubt about the meaning of "handling" in this instance, but when the question was raised with Hetty, she knew it as a molestation. There is much that is sur-

Sipprell Studio advertisement

prising about this story: unless the man was caught in the act of "handling" her, Laura told someone what happened; she was believed; action was taken; and the incident was not hidden in shame but retained as a part of the family's collective memory. Even more significantly, it was written down – by the father – and the assailant was named.

It is not possible that she experienced no psychological or social consequences as a result of that fact. Laura's youngest sister, Mary, remembered her as "aloof" and "stand-offish" during their teen years;[3] that she spent a great deal of time alone in her room; and that, unlike her sisters, she did not date or entertain serious boyfriends. Mary said that although Laura "had boyfriends once in awhile,"[4] none were "red-hot romances."[5] Far from it: Laura "turned boys off."[6] When Lucy and Mary had a houseful of boys in for an evening of singing and dancing, Laura withdrew to her room or went elsewhere rather than participate. One young man who spent a year or so courting her, who shows up in the family photo albums during 1940, and is listed in ACP's journals as present for Christmas dinner along with the boys who would eventually marry Hetty and Lucy, was never really a serious contender. Certainly, Laura is remembered by the next generation of the family as the different one of the four sisters. While ACP recorded what he probably thought were double-dates with Hetty and Jack, double-dates with a future, Laura kept that young man, George Perkins, at arm's length and eventually he settled for friendship only as his role in her life. Mary remembered that George became a member of the family who would stop by the house and stay to talk to her mother if none of the girls were home.[7]

The second of Laura's three life-changing events is a month-long quarantine the family shared in their Calgary home during November and December 1928. They were isolated for scarlet fever – complete with the big yellow warning sign on the door and groceries left on the step – too soon for them to benefit from the discovery of penicillin. There is no way to know how ill any of the children were or what immediate complications arose as a result. It would seem the sickness passed as childhood sicknesses do. But this bout of fever could be the solution to the great puzzle that arises about Laura's health the following year.

According to her public school records, Laura suddenly stopped attending school after November 1929. She was thirteen years old and in grade seven. She attended only twenty days of school during the rest of the 1929/30 academic year, while her sisters' attendance remained high. Her father's journals are uncharacteristically

silent on this point

and, in fact, I only discovered her truancy when I managed to acquire copies of the girls' information cards from Calgary Education. Since Mary was only eight years old at the time, her age may explain why her memory did not note anything out of the ordinary having happened. Rather, she dated the end of Laura's public school education from the third of the three major misfortunes that struck her eldest sister, and supposedly "ruined her life."

Mary says that Laura "was not ever real well."[8] She described her sister as "snooty" and remarks that Laura had an "open the door for me"[9] attitude that her sisters did not share. Laura "wanted to be waited on"[10] and their cousin Jane recalled that Laura was a rather demanding guest during her 1939 solo visit to relatives in the East,[11] a visitor who expected "to be waited on." Likely, Laura's ill health created a cycle of indulgences and demands between Laura and the rest of the household. Her needs and wishes catered to, she began to have an expectation that this was the natural order and her right.

Since Laura was tutored at home and never returned to school with her sisters, whatever afflicted her was chronic in nature. I entertained the possibilities of tuberculosis, nervous or mental breakdown, and lupus – all of which remain possibilities because of their potentially vague and prolonged unwellness (although Mary rejected outright the breakdown theory). However, given Laura's more specific, remembered and recorded, encounters with kidney disease later in life, I suspect that she contracted an infection secondary to the scarlatina for which the family was quarantined in 1928, and that her health was incurably compromised from that date. While still in her mid-thirties, she underwent the surgical removal of a "shrivelled" kidney. From that description (I am told), in all likelihood the defect was congenital and indicates that at the time of her exposure to scarlet fever, Laura had only one healthy, functioning kidney.

Because of this disadvantage, she was susceptible to more severe consequences than her sisters. They recovered, and she did not. Predisposed thus to renal disease, she had the added misfortune to contract an infection which progresses, untreated by antibiotics, to organic involvement. The post-strep complication results in lesions and a condition called polyarteritis nodosa that causes nephritis. It is entirely possible that Laura's death from acute renal failure resulted from her bout of scarlet fever thirty years earlier. It would explain the vague and sporadic unwellness that was Laura's lot in life, vague enough to escape accurate diagnosis or efficacious treatment at the time and severe enough to keep her out of school (with periodic and brief exceptions) for the rest of her life.

The more well-known and more spectacular physical calamity, which is carefully recorded in the journals, occurred a year after Laura's public-school career ended. It was so dramatic that her previous and persistent malaise was relegated to the realm of the forgotten. Ironically, if she pre-

GIRL INJURED WHEN THROWN WHILE RIDING

DRUMHELLER, Dec. 10.—Laura Pierce, 13-year-old daughter of Mr. and Mrs. A. Craig Pierce, of Calgary, was thrown from her horse Tuesday afternoon and upon being rushed to the Drumheller hospital it was found she is suffering from a fractured skull. It appears that Miss Pierce was visiting at Roy Haymond's place which is near her father's large holding southwest of Drumheller and was out for a horseback ride. Mr. Haymond noticed the riderless horse coming home and sensing something wrong hurried in the direction from which the horse came. He found the young girl lying unconscious on the trail. He rushed her to the hospital where she is under the care of Doctors Ross and Sweeney. Her parents have come to Drumheller.

Laura's skull fracture reported

viously had been well, this third mischance never would have taken place. December 9th, 1930 was a Tuesday and a school day. It was also Craig and Adele's fifteenth wedding anniversary. But instead of being at school with her sisters, Laura was at the farm with her father.

On the day in question,[12] Laura took the opportunity to go for a ride across country to the neighbours' for a visit. However, her horse arrived without her, and she was found unconscious in a field, having fractured her skull when her head struck the frozen ground. The incident was dramatic enough and the family prominent enough to warrant newspaper coverage in three separate newspapers. Mary remembered being told that her sister's head was split from ear to ear across the back.[13] Her father and the neighbour took Laura to the hospital in Drumheller.

Her mother arrived from Calgary at ten o'clock that night, driven by a family friend. ACP and MAM spent that night and the next four days and nights at her bedside, leaving only for meals at the home of friends. By the 14th, MAM was "ordered to observe visiting hours,"[14] and ACP made a day trip to Calgary, likely to see the other girls and reassure them about their sister's condition. Laura must have been making a promising recovery since she was strong enough to cause "5 nurses [a] tussle giving [her an] aenema."[15] It is after the "tussle" is recorded that ACP states his wife was ordered to observe visiting hours.

After another three days in the hospital, Laura was moved to Calgary by train on the morning of December 18th. She withstood the journey well, and Dr. Sisley, the family's physician, and their city neighbour Mr. Quigley met the train. After those nine days of hospitalization, she continued her convalescence at home, and she was able to join her family downstairs for Christmas dinner.[16] The lasting effects of her accident are apparently few: there seems to have been no insurmountable brain damage (and apparently none at all to left-brain functions) among the injuries sustained. She took comptometer training in 1940 and worked in accounting at the time of her death in August 1959. If she really could knit Argyle socks in the dark, she had a remarkable facility with patterns, numeric and otherwise. Her ability with language does seem to have been interfered with at least temporarily. Several years after her skull fracture, while at Mount Royal Junior College (the predecessor of the current university) in the fall of 1934 to complete grade ten at the age of eighteen, her grades for Geometry and Arithmetic were 90% and 94% respectively, but her Composition and Literature grades were 52% and 50% respectively.

The following term, during which she completed grade eleven coursework, her Composition and Literature grades improved substantially. When the college's awards were presented, as listed in a city paper of June 15th, 1931, Laura Pierce is listed three times: she won the "Silver medal for general proficiency," the "Eric Sharples memorial prize in senior English," and the imposing "Eaton cup, Patriotic essay". During her time at college, she made her one known friend, Gladys Cotterell, whose father "was President or Vice-President or some big shot with the CPR and had a private [rail] car."[17] No doubt travelling in a private car suited Laura's sense of her own right and privilege.

Laura may have achieved an accept-

Laura with the Eaton Cup

able level of intellectual accomplishment (although never meeting her clear initial potential). Physically, however, she did not fare nearly so well. She did not grow beyond the five-foot-four-inches she stood before the injury, on the short side for her nuclear family, and she had no sense of smell after that, a reasonable result of brain injury sustained to the back of the head. Hetty remembered that Laura was frequently in the bath because she always feared she might be offensive. In fact, she said, if Laura could not be found there was a good chance she was in the tub.

These three blows – molestation, infection, and fracture – all taken within nine years and in very early life, effectively sealed Laura's fate. Somewhat reclusive and frail, in spite of her repeated attempts to redraw her course, she was no match for the hand that was dealt her. Those who say we make our own lives blind themselves to the powerful influence of chance (such as a useless kidney) and the free agency of others (such as the volition of a child molester). If Laura's only misfortune had been the riding accident, her life perhaps would have developed in a vastly different way. She possibly would have returned to school with her sisters and moved in their circle of friends, but as it was, they did not even know the same people. She sewed their party dresses but had no parties of her own. While they were together in the world, she was alone at home, living an unrecorded life.

She is mentioned in no high school paper.

She appears in no high school yearbook.

She was a member of no clubs.

She did not engage in any sports or activities.

Maybe she was stitching.

A 1930 Christmas greeting she received, sent before she was even discharged from hospital after the riding accident, acknowledges that she seems "to get more than [her] share of misfortune;"[18] an acknowledgement that, even outside the family, it was no secret that Laura had notable difficulties reaching farther back than two weeks.

There is a very curious and unfillable gap of six months in tracing her whereabouts from June through December 1939. Laura had been at home for the previous academic year, having withdrawn halfway through a two-year Dressmaking and Millinery programme at the Provincial Institute of Technology. Unlike her sister Hetty, she did not preserve her assignments and projects. Her father took her to the depot, she got on a bus to the U.S.,

and is not mentioned in the journals again

until she arrived home for Christmas, with her sisters Mary and Lucy from college in Pullman, Washington. She was not at college with them, however. Her cousins Jim and Jane remembered that she visited them without the rest of her family some time after the family's 1936 trip east, but their memories are of a visit of brief duration, perhaps a couple of weeks, and offer no clues to where she went next. Six months is a very long time for a twenty-three-year-old woman to travel alone and unaccounted for in 1939. Her sister Mary said an unwanted pregnancy is out of the question, but all families have secrets, even (or especially) from each other. Although Canada was at war during the last half of Laura's hiatus, she was in the United States, which was not, and so she was not engaged in any kind of war-related work.

In fact, she had no career experience or training (aside from seamstressing) and had never had a job. Laura lived at home before her departure and lived at home after her return. If anyone knows where she was or what she was doing during those six months, and whether she was alone or not, no one ever talked. The two most likely possibilities are premarital pregnancy or a sojourn at some sort of spa or retreat in an effort to resolve her frail health. Mary insisted that all four sisters were virgin brides, and I know that is not true. In Laura's case, although pregnancy has to remain a possible explanation, her general reputation as standoffish and as something of a Duchess inclines me to think she simply would have considered premarital sex beneath her. Her personality does not seem to have been compatible with frolics of the unseemly kind.

Even before the onset of her kidney disease and the incident of her head injury, Laura was a demanding, petulant little miss, but it was a spunkier, more fiery kind of forcefulness that somehow lacks the unpleasantness of her later behaviour. There is a charming sequence of letters that was saved from the time of MAM's trip east in early 1928. At the age of eleven, Laura wrote to her mother

> You said I could have that jinger [*sic*] and they won't let me have any. Josephen [*sic*] hid it and I haven't had any for 3 days. Mrs. Kemp and Josephen [*sic*] can just go to ⬇. I want you awful much. Please hurry and write and make 'em give me some jinger.[19]

I was surprised and delighted by this show of energy. Apparently, she considered it acceptable to condemn the hired help to hell as long as a descending arrow is used to designate the place and the actual word is never used, which would be unladylike. But she makes her point. Her mother replies that Laura "must remember Mrs. Kemp is not use [*sic*] to racket and you mustn't drive her crazy"[20] and closes the letter with the "hope you got your ginger, dear."[21] The letter contains no admonishment for consigning Mrs. Kemp and Josephine to damnation. Laura subsequently writes to report that she "had a big piece of jinger tonight to make up"[22] so apparently they saw the error of their ways and sought to atone.

The few samples of Laura's letters to her mother stress Laura's affection and record how anxious she was for her mother to return home. In one of these three letters, she declares over and over

> I love you so much. I wish you where [*sic*] here I'm so lonesome [. . .] I want you so much, Mama dear. I wished youed [*sic*] hurry home [. . .] We're going to miss you an awful lot here [. . .] Oh! how I love you.[23]

Laura must have been pining for her mother because MAM writes to urge her to "Try to eat your meals, my darling. You might get sick. And Mamma will soon be home."[24] Woven through the declarations of longing in these letters is evidence of a bit of a theatrical streak. Laura reports in one that "the fire bells went by. A lumber yard (blew up) burned up [. . .] There was sparkes [*sic*] flying and there was an awful lot of smoke. I'm sending some pictures of the fire."[25] In another she abruptly begins, "How are you? We're all fine. Eva almost hung herself,"[26] somewhat dramatic considering Eva was a caged bird.

In later years, the four sisters and a friend or two frequently would "play act," as Hetty used to call it, mounting major backyard productions in which they would perform both light and serious dramas in costume. Laura was active in these productions and in fact clearly is the central character in this particular presentation that someone

The Pierce girls "play acting"

Laura with her sisters and their pony

Laura with her sisters and kittens

recorded for the family photo album as an example of the girls' stage habit.

During childhood the four sisters were photographed together regularly. When they were little they had a pony at the farm, retired from work in Drumheller's coal mines. They raided nests of kittens in the barn together. But then the contents of the albums change. On a timeline with the change in Laura's health, there are often pictures where she is not. Instead, the pictures include only the three younger girls, something that did not occur before mid-1929.

When the family travelled, the group photographs most often show Laura next to her mother, very often holding her hand. The subtleties of the albums quietly reveal a change in the family's way of being, a split developed, not of affection but of activity, and the four sisters became three sisters and one sister.

Hetty, Lucy, and Mary

The Pierce family, Laura and MAM holding hands

Epilogue

Through her own physical weakness and psychological susceptibility, Laura had a greater sensitivity to those whom her sister Hetty called "underdogs," and as a result, in 1946, she married extremely unwisely. She attempted suicide by a drug overdose while living on the farm with her husband in 1954. They were there ostensibly to help Hetty work the farm after she was widowed in late 1953. Mary said that ACP was well aware that "it'll never work,"[27] but as she also said, "we always knew [our parents] would do anything in the world for us,"[28] and this doomed attempt to offer Laura and Terry some stability is an example of that willingness. At the time of her death, she was estranged from her alcoholic husband (of whom no one had anything nice to say) and living with her widowed mother.

Laura had no children but no one knows whether that was by design or by chance. Maybe her psyche was sufficiently scarred to interfere with her conjugal relationship. Maybe her physical health was sufficiently poor to prevent conception. Maybe her personal circumstances were so unstable that she consciously took contraceptive precautions. To his credit, her husband never approached any member of the family in any way for any purpose after her death; but of course by then he was no doubt very well versed in the stipulations of ACP's iron-clad will (made that way with Terry in mind, Hetty always said, and Mary concurred) which made each daughter's share of his estate untouchable without the unanimous consent of the others. ACP once said "that Terry wanted a rich girl,"[29] which according to Mary was "about the meanest thing he ever said about anybody. He hated his guts."[30] Laura's share of the estate reverted to her mother and sisters.

CHAPTER FIVE

HENRIETTA TORRENCE PIERCE (1918–1992)

HETTY IS THE ONLY ONE OF THE GIRLS TO BE born in Canada, a fact her unabashedly chauvinist mother always lamented, especially when Hetty decided to vote in Canada and seal her fate as a Canadian citizen. The international influenza epidemic of 1918 made MAM's travel across the border inadvisable if not impossible, so instead of heading east to her mother in early autumn, MAM stayed in Alberta, and her mother came to be with her. Hetty was born in Calgary on December 6th and named in honour of her paternal grandmother. It is a rather heavy name compared with her sisters' more lyrical Laura, Lucy, and Mary, and it took Hetty some time to reconcile herself to it. And, while her parents had no problem with what to name her, they certainly had trouble deciding what to call her. Her father's journal entry of January 5th, 1919 refers to her as "Henrietta" when she is one month old, but then she becomes "Baby" again. On March 2nd, he mentions weighing "Torrence," who is a respectable 12¾ pounds at three months, but then she is "Baby" again three days later. They were still calling her "Baby" in May when she was five months old, then "Hetty" is inscribed on photographs taken during the summer, and late in the year a photograph was inscribed "Torrence" again.

Eventually, Hetty said, she realized her name was not so much a burden as a gift, a realization due in large part to her father's uninhibited display of grief when his mother died in June 1926. Able to carry the name herself, and perceiving it to be more a title than a name, Hetty still warned her own children, maybe only partly in jest, that if any of us dared to name an innocent little girl after her she would disown us. She said she loved her name because of what it meant, but that it just was no name to be giving a little girl. It was rather uncommon even in my mother's own generation and perhaps a generation before that. Certainly, I vividly remember being devastated by a friend in junior high who derisively and cruelly remarked that Henrietta was not a people name – it was a chicken name. So far no one in the family has used the exact name again, although I did find a Celtic form to use as my daughter's third name, but perhaps it is due to come into fashion again.

The spring after Hetty was born, the family moved to the newly purchased farm at Drumheller. Conditions in the house were nothing like MAM had been accustomed to, of course, and "on top of this, the baby [Hetty] has been bad ever since we came out here – whines all day long till I am ready to jump over the moon. Also she had such a cold and the matter just ran out of her poor little eyes."[1] She was ill again the following year, and with her sister Laura, spent ten days in April 1920 in the Isolation Hospital with measles. Three months later, Hetty had an uncomplicated bout of German measles at the end of July,[2] and on another occasion, only another month after that, Hetty and Laura both were seriously sick again.

Starting August 20th, while the family was on the farm, the little girls were sick enough for the doctor to be called and to come from Calgary (at least a four-hour drive at that time or a trip by rail), once

Hetty at 2½

for Laura on the 23rd and again for Hetty September 4th, when the call was made at midnight.[3] Finally, by September 9th, "Hetty seemed better" and that is the last mention of whatever ailment they had suffered. The only symptom ACP mentions in the journal is diarrhea, an extremely dangerous sickness in small children. The doctor who had come to attend to the children provided MAM with explicit written instructions for the girls' recovery diet. MAM wrote "Dr. Stockton's Summer Complaint Remedy – <u>Valuable</u>" on the envelope.

We still use the euphemism "summer complaint" in the family, but not the involved five-stage dietary plan which begins with several days of two-to-four ounce doses, given five times a day, of buttermilk and flour which have been well beaten and boiled for half an hour, gradually and occasionally supplemented by adding stale bread, and very slowly reintroducing scraped beef, then curd and barley water, rice boiled for five or six hours, and eventually vegetables and stewed fruit at the last. Treatment would be so much simpler now. After this closely packed sequence of recorded bouts of early illness, all occurring before she was two and most within a five-month period, Hetty was in robust health throughout the remainder of her childhood.

She "started to school"[4] at Kirby School in the country at a most peculiar time of year, February 25th, 1924, and when she was a bit young to be starting at all because she had only just had her fifth birthday. When she arrived at Cliff Bungalow School in Calgary in November 1926, she was placed in grade two. She remembered her first day very clearly, because she was a little bit late and the teacher, known only through the initials "E. S." on the school record, sharply scolded her for her tardiness. Hetty was so unaccustomed to being spoken to harshly, poor little thing, that she threw up on her shoes and was sent home. She did well at school following that unforgettable beginning, her assessments recorded as Good or Very Good all along through primary and junior high school. She and Lucy both matriculated from high school, and Hetty took pride in stressing she had the credentials to have gone to university.

The curriculum consisted of all the courses predictable for academic students: Physics, English, Mathematics, History, Algebra, Chemistry, and Geography, but at that time also included study in Latin. She enjoyed Latin, perhaps because her homeroom teacher from grade ten (one of her favourite teachers) was the Latin instructor for three of Hetty's four years at Western Canada High School. She always said that if a person knew Latin, that person could figure out what anything means because so much language is built on Latin roots, and she often demonstrated this, particularly with definitions of medical terms. She lamented the disappearance of Latin from school curricula. It was important to her that her children understand she could have gone to university but chose not to. Whenever the subject came up in conversation between us, she used the fact both to prove her capability and to underscore her parents' belief in education for women. In other words, it was important both to her and to her parents that she graduated from an academic secondary school.

Her sister Laura's chronic unwellness would have promoted Hetty to first-born status in the family. Laura's illness in effect made her something of the baby in the family, and a permanent one at that, while the next-born child took on the responsibility and position of first-born – concurrently, in this group of four sisters, remaining something of a middle child in terms of acting as mediator.[5] Hetty was a perfect picture of what results from an unexpected elevation of this sort in family rank: for the rest of her life, she was the one everyone in the family (including Laura whose position she had assumed) depended on and consulted, who made her sisters and everyone else in her expanding family feel secure, and she had a marked desire and ability to do what was necessary to smooth troubles over and to avoid conflict. The combination made her the anchor of the family. My daughter, while in her late teens, explained to a friend that, "our grandma is the centre of the universe for us."

Throughout her childhood, quite literally, Hetty never got in trouble, and was quiet enough that while people remember her younger sisters – one of whom was in the same grade as Hetty all the way through high school – they do not remember her.[6] While Mary needed Lucy to become proficient enough at forgery to write parental excuse notes for her, the only time Hetty ever played hooky turned out to be such a terrible experience she had no fun out of it whatsoever and never did it again. She got away with it, but she said the fear of being caught, plus the terrible shame resulting from being deceitful, just was not worth it. During her school years, she was completely uninterested in putting herself forward and neither sought nor held any offices at school, served on no committees, participated in no sports, and is mentioned only one time in the school paper, in a little piece mentioning all four Pierce sisters.

Her sole involvement was as a member of the Debonaire Club, a social group on whose executive Lucy served. This marked absence from extra-curricular activity had a different foundation from that of her sister Laura and changed substantially in her adulthood, specifically in her widowhood. Laura's absence was one of necessity, and Hetty's was one of inclination. She was not incapable and neither was she a shrinking violet. While she was a lady, she was never prissy. As an adult, she took up curling as a team skip and as a member of the executive of the local curling club. She was a member of the Women's Institute, a rural women's lifeline, and was a member of the Eastern Star, the women's organization attached to the Masonic Lodge.

During school, she had a best friend in Doreen Bradley and attended dances like everyone else she knew, but Hetty was already out of social circulation in terms of matchmaking by the time she got to Western Canada High School in 1934. A year earlier, when she was only fourteen, she had met my dad, John Wilson Humphries, who was just turning fifteen. She would explain to us that they were at a birthday party when they met,

Hetty at 14

whose birthday she could not remember, and she fell in love with him before she even knew who he was, before he even spoke. She remembered that he turned and looked at her over his shoulder, arched his left eyebrow, and that was it. Neither of them ever dated anyone else. The yearbook indicates that in the first year of grade twelve her "chief diversions are dancing and Jack Humphries,"[7] but unlike most yearbook teasing on the subject of boyfriends and girlfriends this one was the simple and lasting truth. They had already been a couple for four years by then. Two years after they met, in the summer of 1935, Jack spent two weeks working on the farm, and in 1936, my parents and grandparents even went out to the movies together to see *Ruggles of Red Gap* at the Kinema. In 1937/38 Jack was attending the Olds School of Agriculture, sixty miles north of Calgary in the town of Olds, where Hetty travelled to see him on a couple of weekends when he did not return to the city. He was there to learn the theoretical side of farming. His parents had separated in

Hetty with Jack in early spring, 1936

1936, and by Christmas 1938, my dad, his father, and brother Gord were part of the family at Christmas dinner.[8] In August 1939, ACP and MAM took Hetty and Jack along on an overnight trip to the mountains.[9] Often, during the last couple of years of their courtship, Jack came along to church on Sunday and back to the house for dinner. He came into the family in a more intimate and complete way than do most who marry.

The activities with which Hetty occupied her free time, time not occupied by her boyfriend, that is, were piano and sewing, according to her final yearbook bio,[10] which also states she would be at the Tech the following year. "Tech" was the Provincial Institute of Technology and Art, now known separately as the Southern Alberta Institute of Technology and Alberta College of Art and Design, in Calgary. Piano and sewing are potentially somewhat isolating activities – certainly piano practice is solitary – but neither did Hetty ever situate herself in the centre of attention at parties or gatherings of friends during the 1930s. Her playing was for personal pleasure mostly and also for service. All of my life she would play, sometimes going to the piano quite suddenly in the midst of doing something else, to play a song or two and then go back to whatever else she had been doing. Sometimes she would sit down to play for an hour or two to accompany me singing.

The piano bench was full of song books and sheet music, and our repertoire included Scottish folk songs such as "Scots Wha' Hae," "Annie Laurie," and "Loch Lomond"; hymns like "Now the Day Is Over," "God Is Love," and "Holy, Holy, Holy," the eternally familiar Doxology; popular songs and show tunes such as "I'm Forever Blowing Bubbles," "Do I Love You?" "Zigeuner," "Temptation" (in retrospect an amusingly odd choice to have a barely adolescent child learn to sing), and "The Impossible Dream"; more technically difficult pieces such as "Nola," which my sister Adele especially remembers, and "English Country Garden," which I cannot hear without thinking of my mother. One of my absolute favourites was "The Road to Mandalay," which was our showstopper, because when "the dawn comes up like thunder out of China 'cross the bay" it really did thunder out in our rendition, and my brother Craig also had a very tender spot for "Moonlight Sonata." We always, as long as she was alive, sang a lot of Christmas carols throughout December, which is what John remembers most fondly. Our house was as full of music as it was of books and with just as much diversity. I cannot remember learning how to read; I was born knowing how to read, and all four of us are lifelong readers whose literary tastes are reflective of the eclectic selections on the bookshelves in our childhood house.

The variety of musical genres and the span of musical periods to which we were constantly exposed show how much a part music played in our home life because of our mother's influence. What she did not play on the piano, she played on the record player, and we listened to Ray Charles as much as Chopin and Beethoven, as well as great comedy recordings by Shelley Berman and Bill Cosby. Hetty also played piano for the Christmas concert at our two-room school for many years after we had all left home. It was a way of combining something she enjoyed with her sense of responsibility to perform a community service. As for the solitariness of stitching, while it is very likely that Hetty engaged in quiet hours with her sister Laura, as they both did various types of needlework, she was not someone who spent organized afternoons in a sewing group or who participated in quilting bees. She knitted, crocheted, embroidered, quilted, darned, and sewed (everything from matching dresses for my sister and me to bras and panties) all her life. Every Christmas when our children were young, each of them received a toque and mitts in the stocking, which she also had made. The only needlework she did not do was tatting (lacemaking) and needle- and petit-point.

She genuinely loved making things, just as each of her sisters was to find a creative outlet, and in later life she learned how to make pottery as well. After our father's death, she also wrote a little poetry, which she kept to herself, and which was found only after her death. She was a creative person who spent as little time as possible on housework, saying that if anyone could show her one creative thing about it she would start doing it. Clean and tidy are not the same thing, and if anyone remarked on the stacks of papers and magazines on any given piece of furniture in her house, she would remark drolly, "Why not? It's a flat surface isn't it?" She said she wished someone would design a refrigerator with a slanted top so there would be no way to pile things on it.

Practical enough to can a million chickens, creative enough to design her own crewel patterns and skilled enough to make them, and intellectual enough always to be reading and learning, she could not ever find a place in her heart for dusting. Happily, baking is both practical and creative, and we came home to fresh bread all the time, and there was always a pan of brownies to the right of the stove, it seemed. In 1938, even though she was set already on the path to marital domesticity, when she registered for her programme at Tech, it was not in a course with a domestic or artistic focus. Perhaps she saw the production needs of a farm wife as more industrial than domestic. She certainly considered herself to be a participant farmer rather than housewife only, and I recall her finding ridiculous a printed form which declared her to be a "farmerette" by profession, changing it to read "farmer" instead.

MAM escorted all four girls on a week-long trip to the United States at the end of July 1937, and it is very probable that she was mounting a campaign to get her younger daughters to attend colleges in the U. S., the better to meet and marry American boys. Laura had already completed the first year of a technical course and due to her health issues would not have been a serious candidate for such a departure from her parents, whom she never lived away from more than briefly and never in another city. Hetty had already made up her mind and was enrolled in the same programme as Laura, and besides, she was totally smitten with Jack Humphries by then. MAM had waited too long, and her campaign was unsuccessful where Hetty was concerned.

She had better luck with Lucy and Mary. Hetty started the two-year course in Industrial Dressmaking and Millinery in 1938, the same course her sister Laura had begun the previous year; neither Laura nor Hetty, however, returned for the second year. While Laura's decision not to return most likely was made for her by her health, Hetty's would have a different basis. Not only did she never give an indication as to why she did not complete the second year, she never even mentioned not finishing or even very much about the course at all. I do not know why she did not finish her programme, because even though there was no family shame in not finishing, since none of the four girls completed her postsecondary education and nor did their father complete his, nevertheless, it was not in character for Hetty to quit.

There is no doubt whatsoever that she could have completed the programme successfully: the scores indicated on the backs of her mounted stitchery assignments bear witness to this, and in spite of the fact that the Depression would have affected many people's ability to pay tuition and book and materials costs, it would not have been enough to stop her if she had stressed a desire to continue. Perhaps, pragmatically, she concluded that there was no point in returning for another year when she had no intention of practicing the trade professionally and felt she had learned what she had a practical use for already.

The course description in the Institute's *Eighteenth Annual Announcement*, the equivalent of today's Calendar or Prospectus, states that

> Besides employment in shops, qualified young ladies may look to becoming shop owners or to sewing by day in the homes. Sales ladies who have taken the course are able to give advice regarding the suitability of line and color. Ready-to-wear departments in stores require in their alteration rooms not only skilled needle-workers but also young ladies who are competent to make adjustments speedily without impairing the original lines of the garment. [. . .] The study of textile fabrics which is part of the course is valuable to anyone who is engaged in selling or making women's garments. The instruction is given on a production basis and modern equipment is used in the work rooms.[11]

The first year of study included four-hundred-fifty hours of Dressmaking Shop, one-hundred-twenty hours of Textiles and Materials, sixty hours of Stitchery, ninety hours of Color and Design, sixty hours of Mathematics, ninety hours of Foods and Nutrition, and thirty hours of English for a staggering total of nine hundred hours.[12]

The course consists of many of the same things as a Home Economics course might, but is designed with a view to the commercial practice of the skills taught. Nevertheless, it is very unlikely that Hetty ever seriously considered making a career of her skills beyond the domestic sphere. She is the only one of the four sisters who never worked outside the home, married or single. By the time Hetty entered Tech, there was no doubt whatsoever but that she would marry Jack Humphries. There was also virtually no doubt by then that they would take over the farm together. The skills she acquired at Tech would have had a clear function for her rural domestic future.

Not only was it the norm in the late thirties for young women not to have careers after marriage, but Hetty also had to contend with the personality of her prospective husband. My father was an extremely jealous man, and my mother said that she could not even say hello to boys from school if she passed one on the street when she was in the company of my dad. The simple civility was not worth the interrogation that would follow, but she always remained disturbed by the rudeness of it. The telling of the story many years after the fact made her visibly uncomfortable that she had snubbed someone she knew, an innocent acquaintance, in order to keep the peace. She always spoke very heatedly against jealousy, calling it a completely destructive emotion with no positive attributes. Jack's jealousy was made clear enough to me that when I read during my research the school paper's gossip entry about one particular fellow possibly kissing all four of the Pierce girls,[13] I immediately winced, wondering how much trouble she might have had from my father over such a silly made-up thing as that.

Hetty was not a spineless weakling, and so it is troubling to attempt to understand why she tolerated Jack's stringent control and demands concerning her social behaviour. She told my sister of a time she had decided to end her relationship with him, but Jack also was exceedingly dramatic. He did nothing by halves. Hetty said he climbed a power pole outside her house in view of her bedroom and threatened to electrocute himself if she did not reconsider. I find the image absolutely hilarious at the same time that I more soberly try to picture her sitting inside her bedroom thinking what life would be like with that maniac who was out there up a pole. There is no doubt that she loved him, she made that very clear to us, but she must have had moments in which she saw clearly, to say the least, some of the less appealing aspects of marrying him.

The positives obviously outweighed the drawbacks in her opinion. Often my mother would mention how wonderfully he played the piano, and how she wished there had been tape recorders so we could hear for ourselves. He had completed grade twelve Royal Conservatory Piano and loved jazz piano especially. Het told us with pride that he got 100% on his final Trigonometry exam; he did the same in college in his Economics course. He was involved in sports, playing rugby in high school, and basketball, hockey, and badminton at Olds, and it was always made clear to us that we got our gift for humour and sarcasm from him. The high school newspaper records his biting observation, after a student stage production, that one of the performers "was as graceful as a box car."[14]

While he was a talented piano player and mathematician with a razor-sharp wit, his more sinister side is made abundantly clear in his remark to Hetty after they first had sex. He astutely told her, "Now you have to marry me, or I'll tell your dad," knowing full well she could not bear the thought of her father's disappointment. She did not mention it to me, but she also must have been concerned about the danger of pregnancy, although she may have been somewhat reassured by her unfailingly regular menstrual cycle which had her period start on precisely the day she expected it every month from the time she had her first one. It would have made it much easier to calculate when she was in the danger zone for conception. It seems to me that she was, in this first sexual situation, graphically caught between her parallel needs to please both of the men she loved most.

Hetty and Jack's common career goal for the long-term future was to take over management of the farm. My mother was one of four daughters, so if the farm were to remain in the family, one of the girls would have to bring a farmer into the fold. My father, however, was a city boy. He did have a horse named Toby that he rode over to my mother's house before he could drive, but horsemanship does not make a farmer. In 1935, when Jack and Hetty were seventeen, they spent two weeks in the summer working on the farm with my grandfather; Jack's grooming and training had begun. The following August, 1936, Jack went out to work for the first time without my mother along. He was eighteen and had arrived at that moment of decision about what career to pursue. His younger brother Gord, who candidly remarked that Jack could be rather overbearing, has told me that there was a time when my dad had wanted to be a radio announcer and drove everybody in the house crazy practising his radio voice.

He went to work for a stock brokerage, James Richardson & Sons, in 1936, making $30 per month and was offered a $5 per month raise as an incentive to stay. He liked the work, but, as his brother put it, "decided he liked the dirt better." So instead, he complemented his practical training on the farm with attendance at the Olds School of Agriculture where he completed a two-year diploma programme in one year. He studied Soils, Animal Husbandry (and also Poultry, Dairying, and Blacksmithing), Botany, Horticulture, and Chemistry; there was work in Farm Buildings, Farm Management, and Farm Machinery. Most interestingly, he selected Entomology (which included Beekeeping) as an option; ACP had been a beekeeper at one time. Jack clearly was following ACP's model taken at Lehigh University and by playing on three college teams was as much an athlete as ACP had been. While some of the courses even echo those ACP studied, the primary similarity is the respect given theoretical and scientific preparation in combination with practical work.

During the summer of 1936, ACP and MAM made a trip back East, taking all four of their daughters with them. Jack was furious that Hetty went along and was away from him for so long. The girls knew well that they were being shown off to the relatives, these "four gorgeous creatures,"[15] as much as they were being taken around to such pilgrimage sites as ACP's fraternity house at Lehigh. No doubt it was well understood by all six of them in the closely-knit nuclear family that this was likely the last chance for such a trip as a complete family as the girls matured and got closer to leaving home: Laura was twenty, Het seventeen-and-a-half and already as good as engaged, Lucy sixteen-and-a-half, and Mary nearly fifteen. My mother vividly remembered the travel arrangements. They went by car instead of rail, ACP driving, Lucy in the front seat between her parents because of motion sickness, and in the back Laura behind her father, Mary behind her mother, and Hetty in the middle: over two-thousand-five-hundred miles each way in July and August in a car without air conditioning, every one of those miles in the middle of the back seat for Hetty.

It is no wonder at all that she could remember it vividly. My mother's other strongest memory of the trip was a far more pleasant one for a number of reasons. It was the day she opted to go with her father, instead of shopping with her mother and sisters, to see the Olympic trials in track. She got to see Jesse Owens run, and ACP's pictures of the event are part of the Pierce collection at Calgary's Glenbow Museum. The fact that she went along with her dad, as much as it tells about her lifelong disinterest in shopping, underscores her particular similarity and bond with him in some things. She followed sports avidly all her life, as he did, and she is the daughter who brought him and herself a man who would keep them on the farm. That she wanted to be on the farm is beyond question, really, because both she and my father could have thrived under different career decisions, but elected not to consider other things, and Hetty never would have moved away from the land.

ACP met with the American Consul over lunch in July 1940 to discuss "our status and kids going back to Wash. State & family moving to U. S." and then a few days later "talked to Jack H. re future plans."[16] He was confident enough in Jack's ability to take over operation of the farm to start making plans for leaving Canada to live in the United States again, no doubt at MAM's insistence since he always seemed happy to make his life in Canada. The combined need to reside on American soil and to be near the girls restricted the choice of where they would go, and they did settle on Spokane a short while later. But first, in August, they had to discuss the wedding with Hetty and Jack and have people "in to see Het's presents."[17] MAM had to send announcements, and they all were "chasing around with car shopping" by the 19th.[18] Finally,

Wednesday, August 21st was "Hetty's wedding day. Gathering flowers [from the garden] etc. for Hetty's wedding."[19] My parents had formal engagement portraits taken and these accompanied the wedding announcement in the newspaper society pages. The article reveals that

> The bride, who will be given in marriage by her father, will wear a pretty frock of powder blue with tucking in the bodice and a full gored skirt. She will have navy accessories and a small bouquet of yellow roses and larkspur. Her sister, Laura, will wear a Chinese tea crepe frock fashioned with a low waist line and a full skirt. She will carry a bouquet of ivory roses. The groom's brother, Gordon, will be best man.[20]

ACP's journal entry for the day says that MAM, not Laura, "stood up" with Het. The wedding took place at home at 5 o'clock in the afternoon, officiated by Rev. Ashford, with only a small number of guests in attendance. After MAM "served very fine supper,"[21] Hetty and Jack left for their honeymoon in the mountains from Banff to Jasper, staying in cabins and hotels and visiting all the lakes and falls and icefields along the way. They even wrote a few letters home during the short trip.

On September 1st, ACP "Loaded up Dodge truck with stuff of Jack & Hetty after dinner,"[22] and there were other trips to the farm with a "lot of their things"[23] and a "load of Hetty's furniture"[24] during

Hetty and Jack, 1940

the next month as they set up housekeeping together. Jack did some cosmetic things to the house, such as putting down new linoleum, to make more pleasant surroundings. They spent their first Christmas morning on the farm together before driving in to Calgary to have the rest of the day with their families at the Pierce house. Hetty was the first of the girls to get married, and it was a bit difficult for all of the Pierces to make the transition. Lucy and Mary had gone away to College, but this was different.

Hetty went along in September on a three-day trip with MAM and Laura when Lucy and Mary returned to Pullman for their second year at Washington State, and in mid-November, when the two arrived for a whirlwind visit, ACP was able to write with pleasure "Laura, Hetty, Lucy & Mary all at home."[25] A few days later, Lucy's boyfriend drove MAM and the other sisters out to spend the afternoon on the farm. Hetty had had her parents to herself through the autumn of 1939 when all of her sisters were away, but now Laura was the only one of the girls still living at home. The others were all gone pretty much for good.

Epilogue

In November, 1940, Hetty and Jack were settled on the farm, their first harvest finished and the house refurbished for their permanent occupancy. It had been fourteen years since a family had lived there. In the long-standing tradition of farming communities, there was a "shivaree," a surprise house-warming/initiation staged at the farm.

> About 25 neighbors drove in for a surprise call on Hetty & Jack – A very fine pleasant time 'till 1 A.M. Cards etc. they brought a big fine lunch & Haymond [a near neighbour and old friend] made speech presenting tray, sugar & cream of silver on copper.[26]

These same neighbours saved the house ten years later when there was an electrical fire in the night, a fire that very nearly overwhelmed the impromptu fire brigade. Other than that, and aside from events that centred on others in the family, the major events of the first decade of Hetty and Jack's marriage were the carefully spaced arrival of children. Their fertility was complicated by my mother's difficulty keeping her pregnancies. There was a miscarriage in September 1941 right before her first successful full-term pregnancy, and then a mid-term miscarriage at the end of April 1944, followed by a threatened miscarriage which was staved off in the next pregnancy. Her last two pregnancies, in 1948 and 1951, were uncomplicated, as far as we know.[27]

Because there are no existing ACP journals for 1945 through 1951, it is impossible to know if Hetty had the same reproductive difficulty in her next pregnancies. The only miscarriage she ever mentioned was the mid-term loss between her first two children, a loss which must have been even more mentally and physically difficult than the first. My brother John Ross, named for our dad and paternal grandfather, was born in July 1942; Margaret Adele, named for MAM, was next in April 1945; then Andrew Craig, named for ACP in July 1948; and, lastly, me, Anne Mary, named for no one in particular, in January 1952. My parents had spent WWII on the farm because my dad was ineligible for military service. He had tried to enlist on a number of occasions but was rejected on medical grounds. He was issued a special pin that men who had not been accepted for service wore to protect them from the public harassment and insult that were not uncommon for men who appeared to be healthy but were not in uniform.

He had developed diabetes when he was seventeen. In 1951, when he was thirty-three, he developed Kimmelstiel-Wilson syndrome, which ultimately results in edema, hypertension, proteinuria, and renal failure. My parents had discussed with a doctor before their marriage the likelihood of their children being diabetic and were told prophetically that one in four likely would be. My brother John developed the disease when he was five years old. Our parents had planned to have six children, my mother told me; she had miscarried at least twice, and then our dad's medical complications put a dramatic halt to the family planning. My mother was pregnant with me when my dad became ill, and I was one month old when he was diagnosed. At that time, he was told the average life expectancy was two years from diagnosis to death, and that is how long it took. There were desperate attempts to find cures or treatments, one of which involved sitting in uranium mines in Montana. My Aunt Mary told me that ACP "loved Jack like he was his son" and was "trying to move the earth" to find a way to save him.[28] After a trip to the mines in 1953, which John Ross can remember because he was taken along for any benefits that might be had, our dad was admitted to hospital in Calgary. He died in November after a series of strokes and kidney failure at the age of thirty-five.

As our dad's health deteriorated, young John began to take up his farming duties and was working like a man by the time he was eleven and our dad died. Our mother was only thirty-four years old, and along with Johnny, she had Adele, who was eight; Craig, who was five; and me, who was twenty-two months old. ACP had returned to the farm when Jack became unable to manage things, but then only eighteen months after Jack's death, he too died of a heart attack. We know Hetty went away from us for a brief time after our father died, maybe only for a few weeks, but we do not recall where she went. She never talked about this time to us very much. Her strategy, she said, was to pretend for a long time that he was still alive, in the hospital, and she could get to him if she had to. She started smoking after he died. She remarked once to me that my sister had been so distraught when she learned our father had died that she took her to a hotel for the night, the two of them alone. Hetty stayed on the farm even after these two catastrophic losses, taking a business partner who moved onto the farm with his wife, Pat and Ruth Brown, and they ran their two farms together. ACP's estate left the farm in a complicated joint ownership to his daughters and Hetty faced some extremely difficult financial times, even having to buy the equipment she used to farm the place from the estate of which she was beneficiary. Her endurance was stretched further by her sister Laura's death in 1959 and her mother's in 1961, making four intimate losses in the space of eight years.

She remained a widow for almost fourteen years, though not because she had no offers, and then her business partner died. Faced with enormous decisions, including most importantly whether she could, after all this, manage to remain on the farm, she welcomed the offer of a neighbour for one of his sons to manage the fieldwork until she could sort things out. Hetty and the neighbour's son swept each other off their feet, and they married in the summer of 1967. She told me later that she had always known she could never marry a man who was not at least as smart as she was. Jack had graduated from an accelerated post-secondary programme with an A average, while also playing on three col-

Hetty and Mervin's 25th wedding anniversary, 1992

lege athletic teams. She also would not marry anyone who wanted the land more than he wanted her. Mervin Clark and my mother were devoted to each other for twenty-five years until her sudden death in 1992, having a relationship of great love, respect, and friendship. Often Hetty would say, "I'll ask my friend," when she was going to refer to him about something. Five hundred people came to my mother's funeral.

She had faithfully visited her ailing sister Lucy every Wednesday during Lucy's stay in an auxiliary hospital, caused by the advance of her multiple sclerosis, until her death in 1985, and would wash and curl Lucy's hair. This is an example of the kindness that characterized Hetty, and encapsulates how others remember her as a sister, neighbour, friend, mother, and wife. At the time of her own death, Hetty had seven grandchildren and three great-grandchildren. The number of great-grands has grown to fifteen and is not complete yet. Mervin is our children's Grandpa, only one of them being born before he joined the family, so they have always had him. Retired from farming, he and his wife Kay have all four generations of us into their house in Drumheller after Christmas every year. The home site of the farm is no longer ours, but the land still belongs to us, and, because it was her wish, we scattered Hetty's ashes there on a small piece of virgin prairie. When our brother Craig died, in 2003, we scattered his ashes there too.

CHAPTER SIX

LUCY ADELE PIERCE (1920–1985)

IF EVER THERE WAS A BIG GIRL ON CAMPUS, Lucy was it. The yearbooks and school newspapers from the years she spent at Western Canada High School in Calgary are filled with references to her and her activities, social and organizational. Whom she dated was a frequent topic of speculation and report in the paper, as was what she wore;

and any group she affiliated herself with could be sure of extensive coverage in the campus press. I remember her as the most gracious woman, a woman who moved about a room so effortlessly she appeared almost to be gliding, whose Sunday dinners seemed to materialize on the dining room table without her having spent any time in the kitchen preparing them, who spoke so smoothly and softly in a rich contralto, and who could look utterly marvellous wearing red plaid slacks on her gloriously long Pierce legs. Lucy was five-foot-ten by the time she was fifteen.

Lucy, tall and thin

She was the mildest, most serene-looking woman I have ever known, with the warmest, most loving smile imaginable. I always felt sad for her, in spite of her loveliness, because I always understood there was something to be sad about, although I did not understand what it was, not really. I never cared for my name until the day, when I was in my teens, that I heard her calling for my

Lucy crying

cousin of the same name, and she made it sound so beautiful that I realized it was not such a boring name after all. We adored Lucy. Everybody did.

Lucy Adele was born February 9th, 1920, in Richmond, Virginia, where her mother had gone to join her own mother for the winter and to have the baby. MAM had a brother, Arthur, living there. The baby was named Lucy for her mother's closest friend, Lucy Sipprell. As a small child, Lucy Pierce cried incessantly, to the point that her mother was so desperate that she eventually was driven to pay Lucy not to cry. The deal was a penny a day for every day that went by without tears; the strategy was successful as many parents who resort to bribery have found. The girls were rarely, if ever, physically disciplined, and one remembered instance was

that time that Lucy got her feet wet. I don't remember ever having a spanking, but I can remember Lucy was not to put . . . [You know,] she must have had new shoes. She broke through the ice and got her feet wet, and we came home, and Daddy had her across his knees, and his hand raised, and he was gonna spank her bottom, and somebody grabbed this hand and somebody grabbed the other hand, and one grabbed around his waist, and he turned to my mother and said, 'I can't do it.' The three of us were [hanging on him]. There was no way in hell that he was gonna lay a finger [on our sister].[1]

The kids did get new shoes in late November 1931, according to ACP's journals, so the timing would be right for breaking through ice soon after and damaging the shoes. The sisters would have been fifteen, thirteen, eleven, and ten if indeed these are the infamous shoes, so they were big enough to be a serious deterrent when hanging on their father's arms to stop him.

Lucy's yearbook biography for her last year at Western Canada High School claims she "comes from Richmond, Virginia,"[2] which is not entirely accurate but certainly more exotic to Calgarians than Drumheller, Alberta might be. In truth, Lucy had lived on the farm every spring through fall until 1927, every summer for longer than that, and had wintered in the United States only until the winter of 1925/26. After that, the girls had to be more settled at school, and the luxury of having April, May, and June off from classes in the spring and September and October free before starting school in the fall had to be stopped. Surprisingly, such erratic school attendance in the early years of education, when foundations are laid, did not harm the girls' academic success. Only Lucy seems to have had any difficulty at all, and that was short-lived. She may have completed grade one or some portion of it at the one-room Kirby School in the country near the farm, since Laura and Hetty both had begun schooling there, but Lucy is fourteen months younger than Hetty who completed only grade one there, so it is very unlikely that she attended Kirby at all.

When Hetty and Lucy started grade two together at Cliff Bungalow School in Calgary in November 1926, Lucy managed two months of what may have been a trial placement and then was put back to grade one after Christmas. In fairness, she was six years old when she started grade two, so it was a rather ambitious placement to begin with, one the authorities must have felt warranted in making in spite of her age. Very likely the combination of her age, lack of preparation, and the general upheaval of moving house and possibly schools made the classroom work a little too difficult for her. The setback lasted only until the fall of 1929, however, when, having completed grade one in the first six months of 1927, and then grades two and three in succession, she made up the lost ground by skipping grade four entirely and entered grade five together with Hetty again, a year ahead of her age group.

The two middle girls were then in the same grade for the rest of their public school education. Lucy's academic assessments are recorded as Good or Very Good throughout elementary and junior high school, and she did matriculate from senior high school. She attended Mount Royal College (Calgary's junior college) in 1938/39, probably to upgrade her secondary transcript in order to apply for college admission the following year. Once she had reached high school, she also bloomed into a very involved young woman, luckily having overcome her childhood tendency for crying. She served as Room Representative to the yearbook committee for her grade ten class the very first year at Western in 1934/35. Lucy also participated in interscholastic five-pin bowling during her first year, with her team the "Lucky Strikes," which came fourth in an eighteen-team league.

ACP also enjoyed bowling, so this activity was a shared pastime, one he presumably introduced to his daughters and which "Bill," as he often called Lucy, took to enthusiastically. She was good at it, too, and she was the only one of the Pierce girls to bowl competitively, which she continued to do even when her children were young. She registered for league bowling at Gibson's bowling lanes every year she was at Western Canada, winning awards in both of her grade twelve years: one in 1936/37 for her High Double Score of 489, and another in 1937/38 for her High Single Score of 325, as well as tying that year for third place in Girls' Individual Average. When she was in grade eleven, she also apparently was "very apt at borrowing homework," at least that is the claim written about her by the yearbook biographers;[3] she was so busy, it may well have been necessary.

Lucy was even busier in grade eleven than she had been in grade ten, when she had only two extracurricular activities. In grade eleven, she was on the yearbook advertising staff, bowled for the "Gutter Snipes," and was a member of Girls' Hi-Y. Hi-Y clubs were student organizations affiliated with the YM/YWCA. Each club's goal was

> To create, maintain and extend throughout the schools and
> community high standards of Christian character and to

stand together on and for the platform of clean speech, clean sportsmanship, clean scholarship and clean living.[4]

According to Ken Penley, who attended Western at the same time as the Pierce girls, other students envied members of Hi-Y. Members of the boys' club were considered "big guys on campus" and the "cream of the crop"; they were "good quality people," "all the choice boys."[5] Christian though it may have been in its pledge, the club's membership practice was elitist, whether actively or passively. That is, the not-so-big, not-so-choice boys either did not get accepted or did not bother to apply for membership. If indeed Lucy borrowed homework, as the grade-eleven yearbook claims, her scholarship apparently was not quite as clean as the Y might like. She also got "pretty good at writing [their] mother's name," according to her sister Mary, who also insists that Lucy only ever signed it on Mary's behalf, never for herself. Mary says Lucy "was good. She didn't do anything bad."[6] Her minor transgressions of student plagiarism and of forgery notwithstanding, there seems to have been no harm done to her reputation because she was elected to the executive of Girls' Hi-Y for 1936/37, the year after she joined.

That year, she remained on the yearbook advertising staff and also worked on the "Wit and Humour" inserts placed throughout the book. She was selected as assistant circulation manager for the paper, but the gossip columnist wondered, did the manager "choose her for her efficiency or for his own personal interest."[7] If he did have such nefarious motives, it got him nowhere as his name is mentioned again only once in the same context with hers, and it was just another committee connection, not a romantic one. Lucy was also president of a popular

Lucy as a fashion queen

social club known as the Debonaire Club, "probably the most popular and the most active one in the school."[8] In her final year of high school, Lucy was "Western's number one glamour girl."[9] Her best friend, Bette Burland, happened to be the paper's fashion columnist and observed, "One fad which the girls have picked up quickly and with enthusiasm is that of girdles or those belts, more commonly and less correctly called ski-belts. Lucy Pierce started it."[10] Furthermore, not only was Lucy credited with being a fashion trendsetter, but in May 1938 she modelled in a fashion show at the Palliser, Calgary's poshest hotel of the day, operated by Canadian Pacific.[11] She co-wrote the "Scandal" column for the school paper that year, the same column whose writer had suggested the year before that Lucy was getting the assistant managership on her physical advantages. She was elected secretary of Girls' Hi-Y and took charge of arrangements and invitations for a ninety-five-guest banquet in honour of the Rugby Club to be held in December 1937.[12] Her picture is even included as part of the report, which is unusual for a high school paper.

The previous week's paper, November 22, 1937, had remarked she "prefers boys that are golf champions, rugby players as well as being tall and extremely handsome."[13] While the description was made in reference to one particular boy, it could serve just as well for the one she eventually chose to marry, so perhaps the observation was truer than the writer might have suspected when the teasing remark was made. To round out her campus involvements, she served as secretary of the Students' Council, was part of the four-member organizing committee for the graduation dance, remained a member of the Debonaire Club, and was one of the eight founding members of the school Pep Club. This group not only promoted the rugby team by selling tickets, they hosted dances and organized "pep rallies, snake-dances, formation of a school band, distribution of crests, pennants, and yell sheets, uniforming of cheerleaders, buying of rugby equipment, and [other projects] too numerous to mention."[14]

Lucy's being this involved resulted in the later gossip entry that "It sure is hard on Mush McMurchy because there are so many meetings for

Lucy Pierce to attend. He waits all the
time though."[15] This situation is quite
the polar opposite of that of her sister
Hetty, who was the one always "waiting
/ For the boy with the high athletic rat-
ing [Jack Humphries]."[16] Lorne "Mush"
McMurchy was the extremely handsome
rugby player Lucy married in 1942. A

Lucy and Lorne in grade 12

month after remarking on Lorne's patience, a by-line in the paper refers
to Lucy as a "gorgeous creature" and to him as "that tall blonde rugby
hero with the million-dollar smile."[17] They were such a charmed and
popular couple that they even warranted mention in the gossip column
in October the year after they both had finished school. In a poem published in the paper at the start of her last semester at Western, an
unnamed admirer describes

> Lucy Pierce, so beautiful and glamorous,
> Flirts with the boys, so delightfully amorous.
> She's the belle of Western, and I know the whole school
> Would be lonely and sad, if she climbed on a mule
> And trotted away under some other rule!
> You'll never find Lucy by herself very long,
> For wherever she goes there is always a throng.
> At dances you'll notice the boys crowd around
> [...][18]

and one has to wonder how someone so effusively praised could manage
to avoid, as Lucy did, becoming obnoxiously full of herself. The scandal
column speculates in three remarks in February 1938 on the cause of a
black eye Lucy received in a minor car accident. Sitting in the back seat,
she had been thrown against the back of the front seat by the impact.
Embarrassed by the black eye, she wore sunglasses to conceal it.[19] The
columnist notes, however, that far from losing any of her beauty or glamour, "She looks like Garbo with dark glasses on."[20] The following week,

in a piece on the ideal composite person made up of attributes from Western students, the smile chosen was that of Lucy Pierce.[21]

This is the girl whose extreme desirability is responsible for the coinage of a family exclamation often used but never even remotely understood by the generation following these girls until Mary explained it to me in an off-hand way during our interviews. It was such a part of our family language that it had never occurred to me it might and must have some explanation. It always just was, and that was all. When something goes wrong, when plans are frustrated, it is an appropriate moment in the family to exclaim "Bugger Annie!" Our private expletive originated when a young man who was enamoured of Lucy made the assumption that she already would have a date for an upcoming dance and therefore asked another young woman to go as his companion.

The young woman's name was Annie, and when the boy found out that Lucy had not yet accepted any requests from prospective escorts, he frantically attempted to disengage himself for the event so that he might ask for Lucy's company. In his panic and haste flipping through the telephone book searching for the unwitting Annie's phone number, hoping he was not too late after all to obtain the dream date and knowing every second was vitally important, he repeatedly exclaimed, "Bugger Annie!" in frustration. Unbeknownst to him, poor lad, the woman serendipitously visiting with his mother that very afternoon was Lucy Pierce's mother, who took the story home for the amusement of her family.

The middle-born child is independent, the one to leave home first and to find close companionships outside the family because of the opportunity these situations provide for the middle-born child to emerge from the family pack;[22] this is true for the confident and independent Lucy, who, at eighteen, had a job in the hosiery department at Eaton's during the Christmas rush in 1938 and was working there in May 1939 as well, because ACP had to pick her up from work to see the King and Queen in parade when they came to Calgary. Likewise, Lucy is the one who opted to go away to college in 1939 while her two older sisters remained living at home, in spite of the fact that she had a very serious boyfriend who stayed behind. In order to select the school, ACP and MAM took Lucy and Mary along in mid-August to investigate both the University of Montana in Missoula and Washington State College in Pullman, where they "Interviewed Registrar re Lucy and Mary" before making a "deposit on [their] room at #104 Stephens,"[23] where room and board cost $43.50 each per month.[24] While the norm is for schools to ensure the student is good enough for them, ACP apparently wanted to be certain the school was good enough for his girls.

Initially, Lucy registered as a Nursing student, according to her transcript, but her grades in the hard sciences, such as Inorganic Chemistry, Biology, and Human Physiology, are all C's, and it may be that what drew her to Nursing was its caring aspect. She was a very gentle and tender person by nature, plus she would have had the experience of care-giving with her sister Laura, who frequently was unwell from the time Lucy was nine. But providing tender care by delivering a tray of soup to the bedside or providing a back rub is not the core of Nursing practice, and Lucy was not inclined to the sciences. Part of her original view of nursing may have been formed during observation of nurses, especially in connection with her own health in early 1939, the winter before she started college, when the doctor came to attend her because of her appendix on January 11th.[25] After a week at home in bed, she had a series of x-rays three days in a row from the 17th to the 19th, at which time it was decided she did not need an operation. ACP and MAM had both had appendectomies, so while they would have been concerned for Lucy, they would not have resisted surgery if Dr. Sisley recommended it in this non-acute case. A year later, however, there was a different outcome, and one that may have affected Lucy's career choice.

ACP and Dell stopped in Pullman to visit their daughters on the way to a holiday along the Oregon coast. Lucy was unwell and they took her to see doctors in nearby Colfax on February 4th. She was admitted to hospital that day for surgery the following morning. Her father recorded that she "came along fine. No complications."[26] Two days later, she was "recuperating fast,"[27] and ACP and MAM spent every day at the hospital with her. They took her a cake for her twentieth birthday on the 9th, the nurses brought her one as well that evening, and she was well enough to be discharged on the 12th and go downtown for lunch. On Valentine's Day, ACP and MAM continued with their interrupted vacation, and by the time they passed through Pullman on the return trip ten days later, Lucy "looked better than for years."[28] She may have liked the thought of bringing birthday cakes to patients to cheer them up, and doing the other comforting things nurses did, but learned that a greater percentage of nursing duties involved less nurturing tasks. That reality combined with the reality of her science grades to make the decision an easy one.

The only apparent academic casualty of her hospitalization and convalescence was Physical Education. She had gotten a B in the first term, but her transcript shows an exemption for a substandard grade, thereby barely escaping the F she received in the second term due to her surgery. After she returned to full activity the following year, her grades in Sophomore Physical Education were again both B's. She changed her major to English, hoping to fare better in the Humanities than she had in the Sciences. Her grades in American History are both C's, but she can be excused for having a struggle with American history, her mother's influence notwithstanding, since she had been educated in Canada to that point and would have had a greater knowledge of British history than American, as a result.

Her two term grades for first-year English Composition are both B's, which is a respectable start to post-secondary English. Her Literature Survey grade is also a B, which improves on the C in Literature Introduction. As with History, Lucy would have encountered scholarship in American Literature for the first time at Pullman. Her high school English courses would have been dominated by British Literature. More promisingly, her Art Structure and Drawing courses both yielded B's, and along with her B's in Composition, indicate that she was stronger in the production of language and visual art than in analysis and the sciences, better at athletics than at physiology and biology, better at practice than theory.

Her proficiency in art became her creative expression, and Lucy painted until she became physically unable to manage the brush later in life. One of her landscapes hung in the living room at the farm for many years. Because she had been involved with advertising and writing on the newspaper and yearbook every year in high school, she joined the Advertising Club in college and took a Journalism course quaintly called Country Newspaper, where there was a focus on agricultural reports.[29] In her final semester at WSC, she took an Education course called Profession of Teaching, in which she also got a C. What emerges most clearly is that Lucy was looking for a career when she went to college. She tried Nursing, Journalism, and Education, and earned average grades in all of the preliminary courses for these, but none was a good fit because they all quite frankly were too practical. In a way, they were near misses because Lucy was more apt to shine at work that allows action and expression. In other words, if she had selected Physical Education as the major and pursued an Education degree beyond the introductory course, she might well have had a more satisfying outcome. The same is true of Art, but of course these were not career choices especially approved for ladies in the way that nursing and teaching English were.

Lucy's problem at college was that her capabilities were not so well suited to appropriate occupations for women at the time. When she was in grade twelve, her yearbook bio noted that "she wishes to be a designer,"[30] and her capabilities suggest that wish was an attainable one with a viable future. However, Lucy was not looking for a way to support herself in a solitary life; she had that boyfriend back in Calgary. What she wanted was to find a place to stake out as her own, to describe herself as an individual outside of her family, some way to mark her as different from the other girls. She was, after all, the third of four daughters, and a person in that situation feels a need to create her own specialness. Where last-borns strive for significance inside the family, middle children seek it outside. She had shared her bedroom with her little sister during their childhood while each of the two older girls had her own bedroom, and then her little sister had been her college roommate as well.

Lucy and Lorne at the farm, 1943

After two years at Washington State, Lucy returned to Calgary in mid-June 1941 and for the next year lived more independently from her family than any of the other girls ever did as single women. She was as yet unmarried, but when her parents sold the house in Mount Royal and returned to the United States in August to live in Spokane, Lucy remained behind while Laura moved south along with ACP and MAM. Mary went along as well, but she was still attending college in nearby Pullman. Lucy got a job as an accounting-machine operator, according to her marriage license a year later, and lived in Calgary on her own for the first time. ACP often had "lunch with Lucy"[31] as he passed through the city between Spokane and the farm or was in Calgary for the day on business. Lucy was the only one not present for New Year's Day turkey dinner in 1942; even Hetty and Jack were in Spokane for the holidays. Lucy may have been there for Christmas, but she certainly did not linger away from Lorne. My mother told me that Lucy and Lorne had decided not to get married until after the war, to be sensible and wait.

Then suddenly they changed their minds. On Tuesday, May 19th, "Lucy 'phoned to say she & Lorne McMurchy were being married Wed."[32] Hetty, who was seven-months pregnant, and ACP, who had a cast on a badly broken foot after being run over by discing machinery in the field, got themselves organized and hurried into Calgary that evening. Jack followed the next day. In the morning, ACP "arranged dinner for Lucy's wedding party at Renfrew Club" and in the early evening of May 20th, "Lucy and Lorne married by Rev. Morden at Wesley Church at 7 P.M."[33] The party was very small, with only eight witnesses aside from the principals. The decision had been made so abruptly that the bride's mother and two other sisters were unable to get there fast enough. The groom's older sister was there, but not his older brother, who presumably was already in the military services.

The rush was caused by the reality of war, with no way of knowing when a man suddenly would be summoned to service. Lorne had enlisted in the Royal Canadian Air Force, and in November he was in Saskatchewan for his flight training. Lucy went by train to join him at the end of the month. Just before he went overseas, they returned to Alberta for his leave at the beginning of May 1943. After a brief stop at the farm, en route from Saskatoon, they went to Calgary to visit Lorne's parents. Lucy returned to the farm alone on May 13th. My cousin Lorne was born nine months later on February 5th in Spokane where Lucy had gone in November 1943 to live with her parents during the last trimester of her pregnancy. The baby's birth-weight was an average one, just eight pounds, but apparently Lucy's narrow frame caused her to have "considerable trouble and had to be enlarged."[34] What means were employed in this rather medieval-sounding procedure are not described, mercifully. At some point during the next three months, Lucy returned to Canada to show her parents-in-law their baby grandson, and she stayed with them at least for the rest of the year and probably longer.

During the Allied invasion of Europe, ACP received "Word [...] that 'Mush' is reported missing"[35] after an air raid on Berlin June 22nd, 1944. ACP, Hetty, and my brother Johnny left for Calgary the same afternoon, and the next day spent several hours with Lucy at her in-laws', being there when Lorne's father returned and "learned of Lorne missing in action. Took it very hard."[36] The whole notification process was agonizingly long, five months from first word to last, with wife and family knowing what must surely be true but wildly hoping that the missing would be found somehow alive. A month after the first report in late July, "Dell 'phoned [to the farm] from Spokane that wire received that Mush was lost;"[37] ACP was in Calgary the following day to see Lucy.[38] Finally, in November, ACP was with Lorne's father when

> McMurchy had cablegram from R. B. Bennett saying 5 members of Mush's crew including Mush definitely

> killed – German Red Cross gave names & numbers. 2 saved
> [. . .] To McMurchy's to give Lucy Bennett cablegram &
> spent afternoon, dinner & evening there.[39]

My mother said they always hoped that photographs of the baby had arrived before Lorne was killed, but they never knew. Shot down over Holland, Hetty said, there is a grave for Flying Officer McMurchy in the Canadian War Cemetery at Nijmegen. Eventually, Hetty and Mary both visited the site, but Lucy never went.

Epilogue

After the war, the military survivors came home, and among them was Pilot Officer Jim Jardine, whom Lucy had known well while attending Western Canada High School. His family had lived very near the Pierces in Mount Royal, and he had particularly spent time with Mary. Jim and Lorne had known each other then as well, both being members of the same fraternity and Boys' Hi-Y. Many people they knew did not return; the newspapers regularly carried reports of the missing and killed. It was perfectly natural and to be expected that after his discharge in March 1945, Lucy and Jim would cross paths again in these circumstances, either by a chance meeting in public or a private condolence call on his long-time friend who was the widow of another friend.

Hetty said that it was not just Jim who courted Lucy but his entire family, and in October 1946, the courtship concluded with a wedding. Lucy and Jim then moved to Vancouver in order for Jim to study at the University of British Columbia, but the arrival of two children in rapid succession made it economically necessary for Jim to leave university and find work to support his family. He adopted Lorne Arthur McMurchy, a move he felt very strongly about because of his own childhood circumstances. Jim had been born in India, and when his parents both died, he was sent home to family in Canada. Raised by his aunt and uncle with his cousins, he nevertheless always felt an outsider because he was never adopted and therefore did not share their name.

When Lorne Jardine was almost four, his younger siblings began to arrive. James Johnstone Jardine III was born in November 1947 and Laura Ann (whom her father teasingly called Craig Ann because of the two Craig cousins born near the same time) in September 1948. Hetty said that Lucy blushingly was concerned with what people would think of her, having children born just ten months apart. Jim's work plans in Vancouver after leaving university were not successful, not even the first coin-operated laundromat in Vancouver, and the family returned to more familiar surroundings in Calgary where Mary Sue was born in September 1951. ACP's journal for 1952 mentions Lucy calling Spokane to give her parents her new phone number, Cherry 4-8888, which was the phone number at that house for fifty years.

Lucy always helped her children with their art projects, but by good fortune, the Jardines had a neighbour who was an artist and who began after a number of years to give Lucy lessons in drawing and painting to build on her artistic inclinations and college foundation. Beginning with pencil drawing, she went on to charcoal and sepia, then to oils. She did sepia portraits, working from photographs, of her family and on commission. Her landscape painting was all in oils. Lucy was diagnosed with multiple sclerosis when she was fifty years old, a late diagnosis for this disease which typically strikes between twenty and forty, and a development whose lateness Lucy saw as an

Lucy and Jim with Lorne

135

ironic blessing because she was able to raise her family and launch them all into the world before she was disabled. Jim's health deteriorated relatively early in life as well, and he died in 1975. By the time of his death, Lucy was walking with a cane, and as her mobility decreased and she needed support in the home, Mary Sue with her husband and young family moved into the house to care for her.

This arrangement continued when Lucy became completely dependent on Susie's daily and constant assistance, Lorne's advice and understanding as a physician, and the practical assistance of home-care workers and Victorian Order Nurses. Very unwillingly, Lucy eventually was admitted to the Glenmore Auxiliary Hospital where her care could be managed more thoroughly, and where her medical needs could receive more immediate attention as her disease progressed. When Lucy was unable even to hold a book, her sister Hetty and her daughter Laura would read to her; Jim III and Lorne offered to provide cable television service to the hospital so Lucy's boredom could be alleviated. Hetty drove in to the city from the farm and washed and curled Lucy's hair every Wednesday. Lucy was only sixty-four when she developed pneumonia and died in the evening on New Year's Day 1985. Lucy had seven grandchildren, and seven great-grandchildren have arrived so far. She was the second of the Pierce sisters to die. Two of her children, Lorne and Laura, also have died very young, in 1992 and 2005.

CHAPTER SEVEN

Mary Margaret Pierce (1920–2005)

IF LAURA AND HETTY WANTED TO MAKE the clothes, and Lucy wanted to design them, Mary wanted to wear them. She remembered "frequently changing [her] clothes – wear one thing in the morning and something else in the afternoon"[1] during high school. And when she and Lucy arrived home in mid-December 1939 for Christmas, ACP felt compelled to note there was a "lot of baggage,"[2] even though the girls were home only for the term break. He and MAM had been "looking at luggage for Mary"[3] as a possible gift only the day before. A girl with a lot of clothes needs a lot of luggage. A self-professed party girl, Mary often pleaded ignorance on points of detail about the family, saying she was not paying attention because she was too busy having fun. She was born on the last of MAM's confinement journeys home to her mother, in her Grandma Laura Moore's house at #9 Hurst Avenue, Chautauqua, New York, on October 21st, 1921.

This last baby was named Mary Margaret, which was her great-grand-mother's name, and when she arrived, ACP "got wire saying fourth daughter had arrived."[4] Mary could be the poster child for last-born children, who are generally entertainers, "carefree and vivacious,"[5] and Mary even started her period in a theatrical way. She stayed overnight at a friend's house when she was about twelve or thirteen and was dismayed to wake up and find she had bled on the sheets.[6] Heading straight home, she entered through the back door and loudly "made a big announcement in the kitchen," to which MAM responded simply, "Het, take care of her will ya?" Obviously, the girls in this family had not been taught to be reticent or embarrassed about such things.

Last-borns also can be "spoiled, impatient, and impetuous."[7] Hence, Mary lobbied hard for a bike during the Depression, even when she was told they could not afford one, and subsequently got a "blue bike and it had yellow wheels and it cost ten dollars."[8] She rebelliously started smoking in 1937 when she was only fifteen and continued smoking for a shocking sixty-five years. From early childhood, Mary was making the effort to be noticed and admits, "I was a show off. I was a daredevil," and apparently ACP had told MAM, "you'd better not get too used to having this one around because she's never gonna make it."[9] She broke her arm in the summer of 1930, just before she was nine, having to stay overnight in hospital (the total cost amounted to $12) in Drumheller after the arm was set[10] because she was showing off, "riding with no hands and the poor little horse stumbled and [she] fell off."[11]

Her best country friend, Sam Stockton, shared in her escapades and was just as reckless as she. He got into and out of hair-raising scrapes so consistently that when he was taken prisoner in the Canadian Raid on Dieppe in August 1942, Mary insisted to anyone who cared to listen for the remaining three years of the war that she was confident he would survive to come home, as he did. Mary was enough of a menace herself that she accounts for the only incident of corporal punishment known in the family other than ACP's abortive attempt to spank Lucy over the incident with the shoes. Mary said that her mother "until the day she died apologized to me at *least* once a year [for the time] she beat the bejaysus out of me" because Mary dumped a vat of freshly rendered lard on the floor.[12]

She also had less destructive and dangerous ways to be the centre of attention and took dancing lessons at Murdock's in 1930, the only one of the girls who ever took lessons, and at her recital in May, she was part of a tap-dancing aviators number.[13] Mary remembered that at the end of the performance she was called out to the front and was presented with a

Mary as an Aviator

bouquet of yellow roses from her father,[14] who was in the audience having made a special trip in from the farm to see her dance.[15] If she had not been in love with her father before, she certainly must have fallen in love with him then at the age of eight-and-a-half. Her grade eleven yearbook bio claims that she "spends most of her time dancing,"[16] and the school paper bears witness to this assertion by having her at every dance, most of the time with a different date, who was more often than not eventually one of my uncles. There was a lot of double dating, but never with her sisters.[17] Mary dated all our uncles, especially my dad's brother Gord (referred to as "Hunk" more than once in the yearbooks) and her sister Lucy's second husband, Jim. She remarks with pride, "Jim Jardine had a big crush on me."[18]

Sunday nights most often found the vivacious Mary with "Lucy and [their friend] Margaret Lecouter and the boys,"[19] at Pierce's, one of the many boys present being Gord Humphries who "Pounds a mean piano."[20] They literally would roll up the rugs and dance on the polished wood floors, and with twenty boys and only three girls present, the girls would have been very much the centre of attention and would have danced every dance. Many of the boys she dated or with whom the paper rumoured her to be involved in flirtations have lapsed entirely from her memory. She was linked with even more boys than Lucy, the difference being that Lucy was often worshipped from afar, but Mary "played the field" in a big way. There was no need for concern about her companions because "we were *all* nice kids," and while everyone she and her sisters knew was from their own social class, Mary stressed that "we weren't snobs for heaven's sake. I *am* a snob" with disarming honesty.[21] While Hetty had one boyfriend for seven years before she married him, Mary dated Gordie, Mush, Alex, Den, Larry, Bruce, Wilby, Herb, Jim, Dan,

Mary with a
pick-axe

Stu, Dennis, John, Johnny, Irwin, Harry, Doug, Frankie, Hank, and Frank, in order of appearance in *The Mirror*, plus another two boys whose names the columnists decline to reveal. However, after all that, she opted not to marry any of them.

The girls had social lives to be envied, and while their home life likewise was one of privilege and ease, there was some very human sibling behaviour as well. The story is often told in the family, including by Mary herself, of how Mary more than once would lean over the banister rail and call, "Looocy," and then spit on her sister when she appeared at the bottom of the stairs. It was a stunt that could be repeated because Lucy was guileless and Mary was impetuous mischief personified. But Lucy was innocent, not passive, so Mary would have to spit and run, heading for the bathroom because "the bathroom had the only door that locked."[22] This is probably one of those moments when MAM would try to instil remorse in the girls by saying, "I would have given my soul for a sister."[23]

Certainly, in many ways, they were typical sisters, staging plays for their own enjoyment in the yard and the house, playing something called "Hu Chu Turn out the Light," which consisted entirely of turning off the lights and then "we'd screeeeam" in the dark. Even when they were adults, differences could become heated, although this response was not the norm for them. In March of 1942, when Mary was twenty and Laura twenty-five, they were playing bridge with their parents in the evening after dinner and ACP reports that "Mary & Laura had a 'flare-up' – I gave them a lecture – more bridge:"[24] heated perhaps, but nevertheless civilized. In a more comradely instance, Mary and Lucy once "played [Cole Porter's 1934 hit] 'You're the Top' over and over [on the record player] writing down the words [as girls often have done with popular songs]. Daddy came downstairs and gave Lucy a quarter and me a quarter and said, 'Will you please stop?'" The girls "used to hang on the radio every Saturday night [. . .] for the Hit Parade."[25]

At about the time she started college, Mary fell in love with Frank Sinatra's voice at the very start of his recording career, and she stressed that it was his voice she liked. She was never weak in the knees over him like the screamers were. She was so devoted a fan that when Frank turned eighty in December 1995, I phoned her to offer felicitations on his birthday, and she said she had been listening to his records all day. At the time of the twenty-five-cent anti-popular-music bribe, a movie admission cost a dime at the Kinema, so ACP's quarter was a worthwhile sum to accept. Mary loved the movies and often would walk over to the Kinema at 17th Avenue and 14th Street only four blocks away to enjoy a movie by herself.

After the war, when they were both living in Spokane, she and her mother would often go to the movies together.[26] And, by staking claim to sororities, the counterpart to fraternal orders, she also found her individual way to a share of her father's interests, just as her sisters did. After all, rural life did not appeal to Mary. She "always thought it was boring as hell at the farm. There was nothing to do, [and] it took half a year to get there." While Hetty cornered proprietorship of the farm, and Lucy became a bowler and as compulsive a committee member as ACP, Mary is the only one of the girls to join a sorority during high school. There had been only one at Western Canada in 1934/35, but there was a sudden expansion to eight that resulted from a "disapproval that relaxed,"[27] and in Mary's very first year there, 1936/37, she was treasurer of the junior Alpha Sigma Rho.

After that, along with her best friend Mary Sherman, she was active in the chartered senior branch of the sorority for both of her remaining years in high school. The group's only identified activity, to come out of the meetings hosted in member's homes, is the same as most sororities in their school: organizing and "sponsoring dances, big formal dances."[28] The group's yearbook picture, when Mary was in grade eleven, shows the sixteen-sister group in matching green-and-white checked dresses,[29]

Mary with her sorority sisters
Centre, 3rd from left

dresses that gaped at the neckline when the wearer bent over so that the girls, who made it a big joke among themselves, had to be careful to put a hand to the chest to keep from exposing themselves. The dresses had short puffed sleeves and wide waist bands drawn tight with a criss-cross lace-up tie.

All of the girls not part of the executive committee seated in the front row had ribbon bow ties to complement the waist-line cinch, and they looked altogether innocent and prim, like girls at a country fair in a wholesome musical, as if they belonged in *Seven Brides for Seven Brothers*. Her only other membership during high school was in Girls' Hi-Y, which she joined the year Lucy was secretary and in which Mary served as secretary in her final year, and she also worked on the yearbook advertising staff with Lucy in 1936/37 when she first arrived at Western. When she got to Washington State College in Pullman, she and Lucy also joined Kappa Delta, a sorority which did fundraising for the philanthropic purpose of helping disabled children, work shared by the Shriners to which their father belonged.

Mary was not interested in athletics as a competitor, but as a performer she was very interested in development of the first cheerleading squad at Western. A sorority sister who had come from a school where there were cheerleaders was appalled that Western had none, a deficiency that they quickly remedied. At the time, it was more the norm for cheerleading squads to be co-ed, and still is the norm for post-secondary squads in the United States, and Western's small group consisted of four girls and two boys. Mary was one of the cheerleaders, "conspicuous in their snappy uniforms"[30] that were provided by Lucy's Pep Club. The cheerleaders stirred up enthusiasm by leading students in "Snake-Dances" organized by the Pep Club. The huge crowd of "six hundred to nine hundred students" would wend its way from Western Canada High School on 17th Avenue and 5th Street thirteen blocks to Mewata Stadium on 9th Avenue and 10th Street, "holding up traffic and disrupting street-car service" and "led by [a] twenty-piece band,"[31] all in order to support the school's rugby team. This was not an orderly march, but a rather raucous parade with decorated cars, honking horns, banners and flags, and the school song "Hurrah For Dear Old Western!" as well as the prescribed cheers coordinated by the half dozen cheerleaders along the way. It is perhaps her antics as a cheerleader that are responsible for the fact that she alone of the family missed the visit of King George VI and Queen Elizabeth in May 1939. While all the others and Jack were ensconced in bleachers set up by organizations with which ACP was involved (Shriners and Wheat Pool), Mary was at home "in bed – hip out of joint."[32]

Lucy had waited until she was no longer at Western to get a part-time job, but once she did it, Mary had to do it too, even though she was only seventeen and still in school. They knew their father disapproved without him telling them; "he didn't say one word to us but mother said."[33] But, for these girls, there was a clear difference between disapproval and disappointment. They had the freedom to make choices such as this one with which he might disagree, but none of them would have braved his disappointment. Mary repeatedly remarked during our interviews that "I would never never never do anything to disappoint him"; "I wouldn't let him down. Let my father down? Are you kidding? I would have crawled on my hands and knees over broken glass." Mary "was in awe of him and a little bit scared," not of physical reprisals ("he was so sweet") but of the power of his personality and stature ("everybody respected him") even in his own house. The girls did not have this awe of their mother, but MAM did have a share in their general reverence for their parents, and Mary said "I would cut my throat before I would let my parents down."[34]

Lucy had made the decision to go away to college starting with the academic year 1939/40, and when Mary found out that she could be admitted to Washington State without her senior matriculation, for which she would have had to go to Western for another year, she insisted on going along, as youngest sisters will. "If Lucy went then I was gonna go too,"[35] impatient to be getting on with things. However, arriving in college without the requisite academic preparation and personal discipline, a typically impetuous thing to do, made for difficult-to-accept academic results. One of the most devastating of those results came in a social way rather than an academic one. Halfway through her second year, keen to be pledged to the Kappa Delta sorority, Mary learned "she hadn't made grades high enough to be initiated into K. D."[36] She was so upset she refused to speak to her parents on the telephone during a February call.

But, her grades were not dismal enough for academic suspension, and she completed five semesters, the most post-secondary education of any of the girls. To start, she declared a major in Sociology, but only ever took three Sociology courses. Her transcript reveals a typical liberal arts breadth, with some Humanities and a couple of Sciences, a Music recital option, a Journalism introduction, and two dominant directions in her other courses. One of these was Physical Education, which accounts for five courses, one per semester for her entire time at Washington State.

The other focus, and the one she selected as her revised major, was Foreign Languages.

Mary remembered taking languages and mentioned the fact during our interviews, and she should remember, since they account for the remaining eight course selections. She studied French language at the beginning and intermediate levels as well as French Civilization, Spanish at the beginning and intermediate levels, and took both German and Latin introductions. She would have taken

Mary as a co-ed

Latin in high school, so she had some foundation for her college-level course. All of the language instruction indicates a mind as lively as the Physical Education courses do the body. Mary's level of physical activity from her childhood daredevil days and dancing lessons carried on into her college years and served her well. The variety of languages, instead of majoring in a single language, suggests a rapid-firing mind that needed constant fresh stimulation for the imagination and to keep her attention. Mary would have been interested in the idea of being in places where the languages were spoken, far more than she would care for the painstaking labour of mastering the syntax and vocabulary of a sole second language. She said more than once that she was there to have fun, and her sampling of several languages exemplifies her predilection for enjoyment and for life in the moment. Her course selections during those five terms at college demonstrate her constantly moving attention, a basic component of her personality.

While Mary was at Pullman, she was introduced by a Kappa Delta sorority sister to Pike Conover, a fellow student from Coeur d'Alene,

Mary and Pike, 1942

Idaho. Their first date took place March 7th, 1942 when Pike unexpectedly called Mary to ask if she would like to go along with him to visit the mutual friends who had introduced them.[37] They drove from Spokane to Walla Walla, stayed overnight with the friends, and returned the following day. By November, when Lucy was on her way to Saskatchewan where Lorne was taking flight training, Mary was on her way to Baltimore to marry Pike, who was in the army and on his way through Officer Candidate School.

ACP had not met young Henry Conover, a fact which speaks to the security of the girls in their father's affection, for marrying a man one's father had never met was not a minor matter, even in time of war. While ACP had not laid eyes on him, MAM "thought Pike was the cat's pyjamas."[38] Mary had just turned twenty-one before she left for Baltimore so required no parental permissions on her marriage documents and, exactly one-month after her birthday, she and Pike were married November 21st, 1942. Together, they had a visit home to Washington and Idaho at the end of February 1944, then Pike returned east and Mary went north to see her sisters before rejoining him in Baltimore. They were still in Baltimore on D-Day, and woke up in the morning to the sound of newsboys calling out a special edition of the paper. Mary remembers her relief that "D-Day had happened and he wasn't in it."[39] Everyone knew the invasion was coming and it was a relief when it finally happened. Immediately after that, however, Pike got his orders, and by the end of June he was in Europe serving under General Patton. He was promoted from First Lieutenant to Captain by the time he came back after the war was over.

Just like Lucy, Mary conceived her first child immediately before her husband went away to war. Mary Allison was born in Spokane, where Mary had gone to stay with MAM and ACP, in February 1945. The baby obviously was named for her mother, and also was given the family name Allison, which was her great-grandmother's maiden name. After the war, the next baby was Joseph Craig, named for both of his grandfathers, who was born in Coeur d'Alene in December 1947. The last of Mary's children is Mary Candace, who is almost nine years younger than her brother. Candi was born in July 1956 after Mary and Pike had moved to Seattle. Pike had insisted that both of the girls be named after their mother. Neither of them is called Mary, however, and all three children are called by the middle name, as are all of the children in Hetty's family – except of course for John Ross, who is called Jack – and as MAM and ACP both were as well. In the years when Allison and Craig were small and before Candi was born, Mary and Pike lived in Spokane and so were very near MAM and ACP, and Laura and her husband, Terry.

It was a fortuitous thing that Mary was close by because during these years, Mary was an indispensable help and support to her parents. While ACP's journals for 1945 to 1950 do not survive, the content of those for 1951/1952 relate countless helps Mary provided for her parents. MAM and ACP were in their late sixties by then, yet still under an unusual burden of responsibility for Laura, their first-born daughter who was in her mid-thirties. Laura had married in 1946, but her combined marital and health problems kept her quite dependent on her parents who occasionally had serious health concerns of their own and who, because of all these factors, were in turn quite dependent on Mary for very practical things. Her chauffeuring duties alone, while she also had to tend to two young children, occupied a substantial amount of time as well as physical and emotional energy.

The day after Christmas 1950, Laura had surgery to repair an obstruction in her left kidney, which had caused it "to distend to 15 times normal size. Probably was that way from birth."[40] The next six months were a constant whirl of serious illness for MAM, ACP, and Laura, with Mary at the helm of all things practical then and for the rest of the year at least. Her parents both had serious bouts of flu almost immediately following Laura's year-end surgery, and her father did not recover quickly. For two months, he was ill with flu in spite of his physicians' best efforts. He developed phlebitis for which he was hospitalized in April, at the same time that Laura had been readmitted to a different hospital for major surgery to remove her dysfunctional kidney.[41] ACP recorded in his journal that "Mary took me to hospital and Dell to see Laura and me."[42] She took him to Sacred Heart, went to get her mother to visit him there, and then drove her over to Deaconess to see Laura, and that is the way her spring went.

ACP recovered and was out of hospital in time for Laura to be taken home, but very suddenly developed nephritis himself in early May, and the family was summoned from Alberta (in the case of Lucy, Hetty, and Jack who drove) and Pennsylvania (in the case of ACP's brother Audley who flew). Mary spent much of her time behind the wheel of her car chauffeuring people about, especially since MAM did not drive. From May 12th to June 20th, ACP had private nurses around the clock; with one exception, his diary is blank from May 16th to August 1st when he is once again discharged from hospital. The exception is May 21st, when "the girls got Laura into Mary's car and all four came to Sacred Heart Hospital to see me – this being my birthday – 67 yrs. Laura in wheel chair."[43] Three days after ACP got home, MAM had a cardiac event of some kind, "was in bed all day with severe pain in chest" for which the doctor prescribed painkillers and sleeping pills.[44] The journal is blank again for the next month and then ACP records that his doctor will not allow him to drive to Canada alone because of his health, so in early October, Jack is summoned to Spokane by train in order to do the driving.

Mary made Sunday dinner more often than not and picked up and delivered everybody everywhere constantly for months, and with a child or two in the back seat of her car while she did it. Undoubtedly the real possibility that her sister and both of her parents would die all at once, the self-described incompetent one actually was the anchor which kept the family functioning at all during 1951. Not surprisingly, she was the one in charge of Christmas dinner that year for all the family living in Spokane. Laura and Terry never hosted anything, always the guests at Sunday dinners at MAM's and Mary's. She must have felt at times that if she could just drive fast enough and cook enough turkey, everything would be all right.

The unfortunate thing about the way last-borns see themselves is their perception that their older siblings have "all the talent, ability, and smarts,"[45] and Mary is far from being an exception to this. Her school records for grades one through eight all indicate Good progress. Another contributor to her poor intellectual self-esteem is the fact that Mary's left-handedness was a physical reality that was not desirable when she was a child, and she remembers having her left arm tied down at school in an attempt to force her to become right-handed. She began to develop a stammer, and her parents put a stop to the practice of binding her arm. She describes herself as "dumber than a bucket of rocks" when she went off to college, and insistently reaffirms this conviction by saying, "I'm telling ya, I had no business being there."[46]

The problem at college was more one of unfinished preparation rather than lack of capability: Mary had not graduated from high school, plus she had had the same emphasis on British history and literature that Lucy found to be a problem in an American college. Sophisticated diagnostic tests to identify learning style likely would have benefitted Mary a great deal as well. She mused late in life that perhaps she demonstrated an attention deficit disorder. She often remarked that her sisters were so smart, that they (and Laura in particular) "oozed talent." Even in adulthood, she "always felt kind of inadequate because my sisters were so talented. [. . .] I was just a klutz. I couldn't do anything like [their sewing]. I wasn't accomplishing anything."[47]

Thankfully, when she was fifty, Mary found a creative outlet that disproved her self-deprecating perception in a practical way. After she, Pike, and Candi relocated to Gaithersberg, Maryland in 1971, for Pike's term as Assistant to the President of The International Brotherhood of Electrical Workers, Mary answered a newspaper advertisement and started taking classes in glass work as a way to meet people in a new community and because she loved leaded glass. I have a few small pieces she produced, and my sister has a lampshade, things that belonged to our mother. If Mary felt she could offer these to her older, supposedly more talented, sister, she obviously had some confidence that she now finally was accomplishing something.

She did quite a lot of leaded glass, but when she got "tired of cutting glass"[48] she turned to another handiwork. For her, creative production with a material result was the measure of success as compared with her sisters. After all, she was measuring herself by people like her sister Laura who could knit Argyle socks in the dark. Mary had a friend who had learned braiding, and Mary, in her own words, "got carried away"[49] once she discovered it. Starting with chair pads, she eventually graduated to rugs and made large, nine-by-twelve foot rugs for herself and each of her three children. She loved this craft. She made my mother a braided Christmas wreath, which I now have, and which I hang on my front door each year.

When Mary returned to Washington state in 1976, she first exercised her creative self by renovating a house, and then earned her real estate license and became a salesperson in 1978. And, she did not merely become a salesperson; she became an extremely productive one. During her real-estate career, she won awards for sales, both in the sheer volume of houses sold and the gross value of the property sold. She worked very hard, produced a lot, and then predictably got "burned out," so she quit. This development is a larger example of what happened in the case of Mary's glassmaking: discover it, do it compulsively, lose interest, then move on to something new or "burn out."

Epilogue

Mary felt the absence of her sisters very hard and of her parents too. She was the only remaining Pierce girl for over a decade. In keeping with her self-perception, Mary was afraid for all of those ten years that she would be expected to know things, especially about the family, since she was the only one left. She said that at times she was distressed to think that some details are lost, and that she should have paid more attention. She felt inadequate to what she believed to be the responsibility of being the last one. At one point during our interviews, she remarked in surprise, "I didn't know I could remember,"[50] When Lucy died, Mary and Het had each other to know what it was that had been lost, but when Hetty died, Mary had no more sisters with whom to grieve.

She and Pike were married for more than fifty years, a family record so far, between deaths and divorces, and they must have been quite a lively pair. Late in life, when he was over eighty, Pike got irate with a highway patrolman who tried to keep him from driving after exhibiting some health difficulties including a blackout, and Pike's response was to put the car in reverse and ram the police car. For five years after his death in March 2000, Mary continued to live in their house with the devoted assistance of her three children, all of whom lived nearby, and her three grandchildren. She missed her sisters. I think it is not a good idea to be the last one left. Not long before her own death in December 2005, Mary remarked to her caregiver that she was going home to her sisters before Christmas.

The Family Circle, 1936

APPENDIX A

These examples of ACP's journals include the first and last entries in the collection, as well as a few of the pages quoted in the preceding chapters. They demonstrate some, but by no means all, of the range of topics he felt worth noting.

30 Dec 1918

22 Jun 1921

28 Jul 1923

06 Jul 1925

MAY	SATURDAY 3	(123-242)	1930

Bob 75 ref.
Bill. Harrow & seeding Reward.
Tom cleaning seeder & garden.
Mac chores & treating Reward.

Fine day - cool.
To Calg. for supper & saw Mary in murdock dances.

03 May 1930

DECEMBER	SUNDAY 17	(351-14)	1933

At Church with Mrs. Edwards at Wesley.
At Whethams in evening.
Mrs. Edwards here.

Warm during day but turned very cold between 7:30 & 9:00 P.M.
Dropped 50° in 1 1/2 hrs.

17 Dec 1933

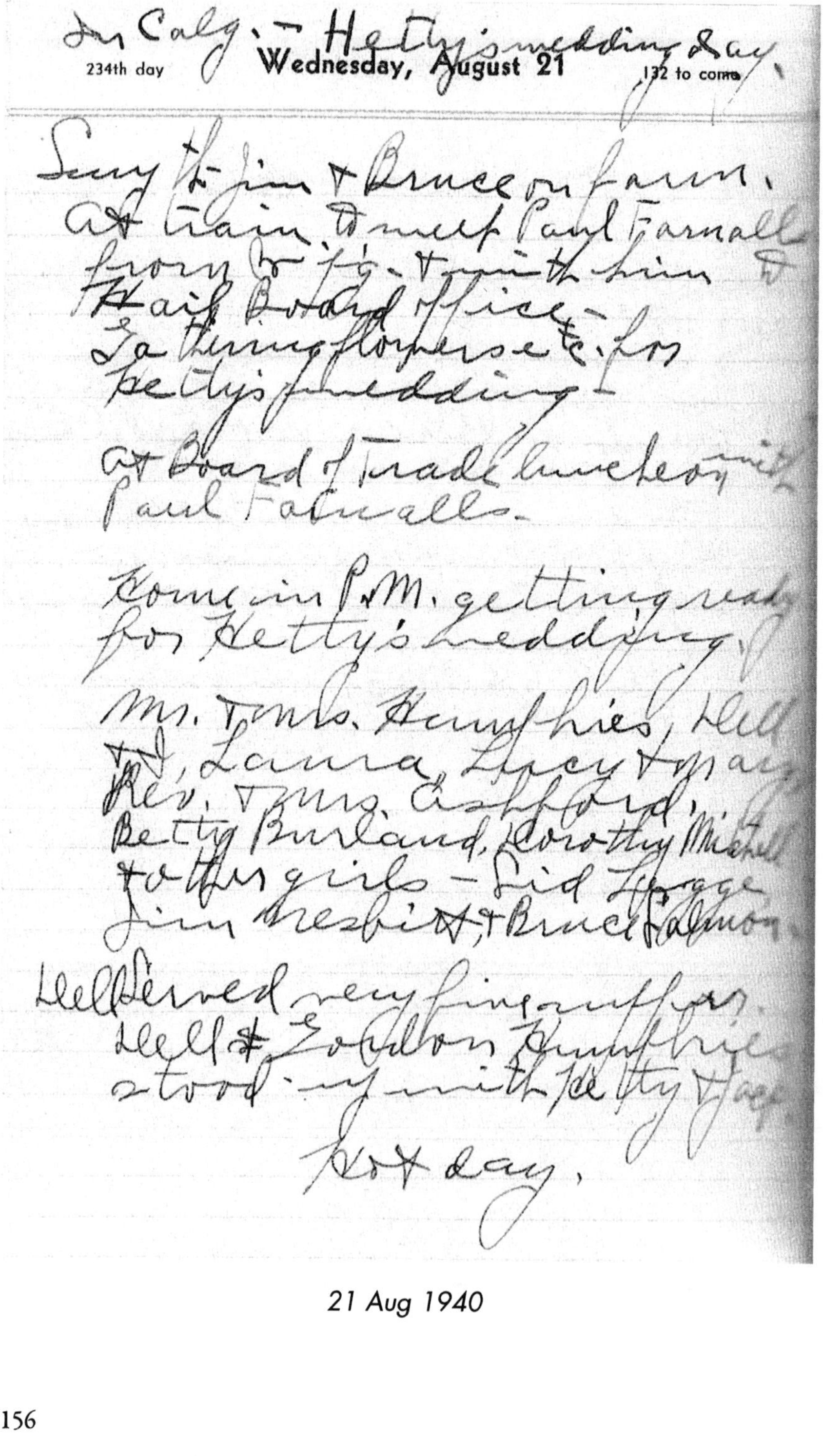

In Calg. — Hetty's wedding day.

234th day **Wednesday, August 21** 132 to come

Sent to Jim & Bruce on farm.
At train to meet Paul Farnall
from [illegible] & with him to
Hail Board office -
To [illegible] for
Hetty's wedding -

At Board of Trade luncheon with
Paul Farnalls.

Home in P.M. getting ready
for Hetty's wedding.

Mr. & Mrs. Humphries, Nell
[illegible], Laura, Lucy & [illegible]
Rev. & Mrs. Ashford,
Betty Burland, Dorothy Mitchell
& other girls - Sid [illegible]
Jim Nesbitt, & Bruce Salmon.

Nell served very fine supper.
Nell & Gordon Humphries
stood up with Hetty & [illegible]

Hot day.

21 Aug 1940

176th day *Farm* **Saturday, June 24, 1944** 190 days follow

Smyth- diesel & one-way finished S.E. 16 at noon, & started south 40 acres in N½-16.

Jack- chores, odd jobs A.M. - on 2 ton & weeder P.M.

A.C. - 2 ton & rod-weeder on north 40 of N½-16 A.M.

Word from Steve that "Mush" is reported missing. Also Hett & Mary phoned from Shop around at noon.

Hetty, Johnny & I left in Pontiac for Calg. at 3 P.M.

News of tornado & great damage in McKeesport.

24 Jun 1944

Spokane

Saturday, January 19, 1952

19th day—347 days follow

Mrs. Onstine phoned
re bridge — they came here.
He was outspoken about
poor cards he held. We
won 1.50. Have always
been + with them —

Jack phoned from the farm
to say Betty had an 8 lb. 4 oz.
baby girl at Drumheller
hospital at 10 p.m. Her
and baby both fine — baby
a perfect specimen with
no blemishes —

19 Jan 1952

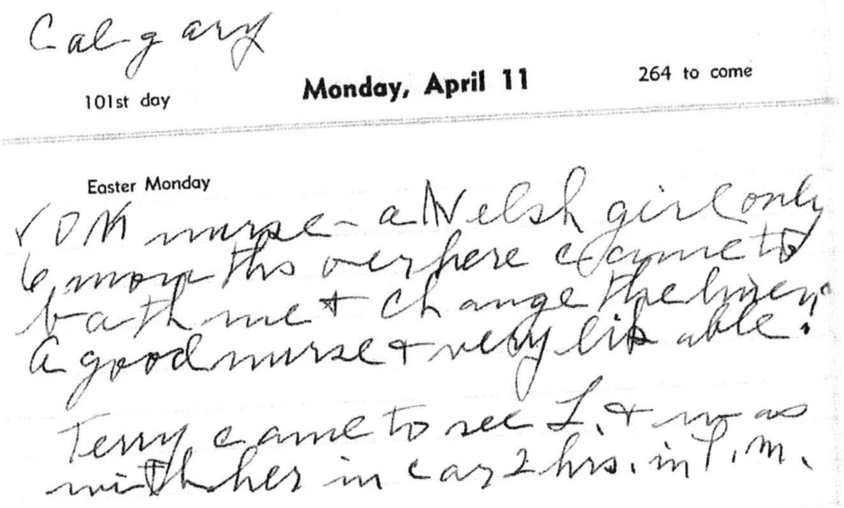

Calgary
101st day
Monday, April 11
264 to come

Easter Monday

[handwritten journal entry]

11 Apr 1955

APPENDIX B

By contrast with ACP's thirty years of journals, only six of MAM's letters survive, but they are a powerful six. They are surprising in their candour and revealing in their details. These reproductions show, in a way nothing else could, vivid glimpses of a woman's life a century ago.

OCTOBER 1916

Thursday Morning.

Dearest Pearl. I was so glad to get your letter yesterday. had been intending to answer the other one but was too flustered to do any thing as the time drew nearer for my Craig – and at that he got here days before I expected him.

I got a telegram Saturday Morning that he would be here at noon – I got fairly silly with excitement by the time he landed. He looks just fine and I am more than a little loony about him. Really I think it is almost suffering to care so much – I want him with me every minute and he had to leave me early Tuesday Morning (4 oc) to go to

Toronto on business. I had a wire last night saying he would be back today and I am all excited again. He is much surprised to find the baby so well developed intellectually. I guess he expected a soft little lump of dough and instead found a human being who knows what she wants and recognizes her folks. She just beams on Craig and says goo at him. I didn't expect him to take to her right away. I mean pick her up and know how, but he acts as if he had raised a large family - knows exactly how to handle her. Oh you wait till you get yours and you will be as foolish as I am. I do hope you get your boy but

Maybe you will get the twins. Craig and I are glad now we didn't as Laura is a hand full. She isn't one of your quiet sleepy babies but a regular buster – never still except when she is asleep. You are a peach to invite us down but I expect you know by now we aren't coming.

I thought it wouldn't be sensible when Laura is so easily upset but I was willing to leave it to Craig. However when he saw her and heard her cry with the colic etc he said "No chance." Home is the place for her at present. I am in hopes of getting her in better habits and have been a little better pleased the last two days. She has slept more and not seemed to have quite so much indigestion. I attribute this to one bottle of malted milk a day which I have been giving her now since Monday. That is a good thing to know. a girl here who had the same trouble told me about it. Then you aren't scared to death all the time that you will have nothing to give them if your own milk gives out for any reason. You know some times if you get nervous or some thing happens, your milk will be affected right away. Mine did last Saturday when Craig came and I had hardly any all day but it is back full force now. leaking all over the place.

I am so glad you are feeling like yourself again. you probably will from now on, feel better & better.

You say you are not
dreading the ordeal any
but that you probably will
as the time draws nearer.
Cheer up — I don't believe
you will at all. I thought
less and less about it
and the day she was
born I never had a
single fear or anxious
moment. Was perfectly
happy the whole time to
know it was so near
over. I made a joke of
the pains till the last ones &
then you get too busy working
and tired out between, fairly
doze off in the intervals — My
nurse told me I would but I
didn't believe her till I did it.
My Goodness but I do wish I
could see you — There are forty
things I would like to say.
Wish you could come up with
Mother Pierce — I suppose you

would hate to lose the time at school but I do think you are so sensible to teach while you can. That money certainly isn't to be sneezed at. Wish there were some way I could help out but I am no good now at any thing but mothering. I do wish it were possible for us to go down to see you all but it wouldn't mean only you. Harriett wrote and invited us there and my brother in Monongahela, the folks in Kittanning etc would be furious if we didn't go there. This would be too much for the baby. She is too erratic as yet. Well. I must close now and see what these grunts mean. Write soon and do come up if you can. We have 18 inches of snow but I am hoping they won't stay. I haven't been out since Monday. Don't dare risk a cold now. Lots of love to you all. Yours, Dele.

October 1916

Wednesday

Dear Pearl. I have been intending to write you ever since my party but had so many letters I had to write that I didn't get around to it. Of course I write my beau every day and got so many flowers it kept me busy acknowledging them. Really it is wonderful how kind people can be. People I never even dreamed of sent flowers to me and Laura got several boxes of rose buds addressed to her own little self. That reminds me, you spoke of her as Louise and it is Laura, for Mamma. I wanted to tell you how sorry I was you were sick. Mother Pierce wrote that you were so miserable. It must go hard with you when you have always been so well.

After my third month I began to feel better and never felt really badly again, only with the heat. Pearl, I want to tell you that I believe that Tokology is the right dope. I didn't hear of it till I was about six months along but from then on I did follow it pretty conscientiously - ate hardly any meat and just scads of fruit. When I got hungry instead of eating solids I filled up on fruit - ate apples by the ton - and you know how I kept going whether I felt like it or not. I went up and down stairs on all occasions and I never got so big that my skin was uncomfortably tight. You have the advantage of me in being able to do more th— I t—

against me. Nor I consider
that I had a perfectly
wonderful confinement. I
woke up that morning (four
weeks ago today) with a
feeling just as if I were
getting unwell. I always
had some cramps but
not severe, at that time.
Well, these cramps lasted
about two hours, coming
every 15 minutes, before I
really thought there was
something doing. Then I

decided I had better tell Mamma
so I got up and then discovered
a little blood so was convinced-
Told Mamma, dressed, got breakfast,
called up the garage and
hospital and wrote Craig all
before 9:30. Happy as a lark
to think the long wait was over.
It never entered my head to
be excited or scared - just all
seemed natural and oh so welcome.

We got to J— about 11:30 + Dr. Perkins examined me and said dilation had started and that the baby's position was right (head first) I never had another pain till 4 o'c— Then they started again just like the unwell feeling— I flowed all day— I wrote Craig again, finished reading Jaffrey, went down to the phone (everyone heard I had gone and kept calling up) I was perfectly comfortable all aft. noon + Evening. At 10 o'c the nurse started to prepare me, bath, enema etc and we made a joke of it. By 10:30 I began having the real pains and at 12 I went down stairs to the delivery room — walked so fast the nurse said she could hardly keep up with me—.

I had asked her before this to send for the doctor and she disdainfully told me she would send when the time came. She told me afterwards she thought on account of my age & being a first only I couldn't possibly be sick under 24 hours but I knew I was having the last pains. They were right at the opening when I went down stairs. I got on the operating table and that is the last I knew. The nurse just took one look & flew for the chloroform. They were afraid it would be over before the doctor got there. I never knew it when the baby came or anything much till I was back in bed. It was certainly wonderful. My throat hurt worse than any place else when it was over. They said I worked so hard to bear down that I rasped my throat. There is no discomfort afterwards worth mentioning.

I tell you all this so you will know what it is like and not dread it. I did dread it and now it is over I would not worry at all about the next one. It certainly paid me to take care of myself though. The other women there had eaten unwisely & had great big babies, two were still born because they were so big. My little Laura only weighed 7 pounds but she is gaining very rapidly and pretty as a picture. She gained a pound last week! You are so lucky that you will have Will with you when the time comes. I almost broke my heart wanting Craig after the baby came. I lay there at the hospital and cried every day just wanting him so. But now I am strong again and he is coming soon so you can imagine I am wild with joy. He is pretty crazy, too — Think of it — he won't see Laura till she is 8 weeks old. Craig & I went to see Chin Chin in

New York when we were just
married (The night before)
It was fine. I'm glad
you are going. Wish we
could see it again.
I've written such a long letter
that I had better quit or
you will be worn out.
By all means have a
special nurse. I had one
two weeks and it meant
comfort. The baby cost
$125 all told. No...

Any thing in the world you
want to ask me and I can
answer. I will be only to
glad to— I would have
been glad to have had
any one to ask who had
had recent experience.
My but I wish you could see
the baby! She is sweeter every
minute— No words could describe
the tender appeal of her.
She smiles and shows 3 dimples.
Where did she get a dimple in
her cheek? Write when you can.
Love to you all. Yours. Dell.

NOVEMBER 1916

Tuesday A. M.

Dear Pearl —

Well! your letter just came
and I am so anxious to
talk to you that I am
sitting right down in the
midst of everything to at
least start a letter. Our
water is frozen this morning
and I couldn't even bathe
Laura — Have last night's &
this morning's dishes hanging
over me (and don't know
when I'll get water to do
them. No gas for days —
Have been cooking on
the electric grill which does

two things at a time
and broil steaks on the
fire place (delish!) bake
dumplings (Craig's favorite
dessert) in the door of
the furnace & get along
some how. The water being
frozen is the last straw—
I could just about cuss
but instead I sit me
down to talk about the
most enthralling subject
in the world — babies.
I can't talk about any
thing else so I am
glad you are interested.
I wish you could see

Laura for she is an
inspiration — Such a little
duck you never could
imagine. She is lying
here beside me on the
drawer post grinning up
in the air (at nothing.
I think she sees things
that aren't visible to our
eyes — I hope to send
you her picture soon
though it isn't took yet.
My chum (from Buffalo) is
a photographer, I think of
exceptional ability — She is
perhaps not so strong on
technique as that she
has the power to get the

real person. Her pictures of Mamma are wonders, I think. Well, she is coming down over Sunday and her beau-lover is coming, too. He is a regular photographer and taught her all she knows. When Laura was born he wrote and asked to make her first pictures as a birthday present. They have been coming and coming and now I guess they actually will land next Saturday — If between them they don't get a picture of Laura worth having I will be very much surprised.

She is the prettiest baby I
ever saw and has so
many cute ways – Sings
most of the time when she
is happy – just a little
high hum but too cute
for words – has some thing
new now nearly every
day.

Oh I wish I could see
you and tell you any
thing you want to know
that I can! I do wish
I could see you before we
go west but we are
going the first of March.
Please have Will let me
know as soon as the
baby comes as I will be

so awesome — You are doing your own work and I think that is splendid exercise & I wouldn't worry about the walking. I went up and down stairs & hills right up to the last — you burn the hill from the dock up to the Post Office — I went up that about every day. My last day before I went to the hospital I went to a party up on the Commons which was up three long, dingy flights of stairs — May have hastened matters a little I don't know. Feel fine anyhow.

After I began my labour the next morning I went up & down stairs half a dozen times getting ready to go to Jamestown & after I got to the hospital I went up & down stairs several times after a drink & to answer phone calls, etc. I thought it might help.

I would not hesitate one minute about going to the hospital. I guess they never had a more tranquil patient than I was. I didn't have worry — just placed myself in their hands — Some times I think it was

Kind of remarkable that
I was so placid the
night she was born – you
know Mamma was asleep
and I was absolutely
alone most of the time
and the rest of the
time with two entire
strangers – had never
seen either the doctor or
the nurse before – Make
them give you chloroform.
If your doctor doesn't,
get one who will – There
is no necessity to endure
the last hard pangs – I
don't know anything about
them – didn't even see
the doctor – They had me
under before he got there.

I had a private nurse but nobody else in that hospital did and it really isn't necessary – I only did it because Craig insisted but I could have got along all right. My bill for her was $50 & $10 for her board – My own bill was $15 a week for my room & that included attention from nurses & board – My doctor only charged $25. The whole business was a little over $125, including private nurse & automobile. You have no worries about household affairs and Ruth the baby is in competent hands.

Most Maternity hospitals prefer to dress the babies in hospital slips. They are coarse and all that but it simplifies matters a lot and you can dress him all you want to when you get home. I didn't really know what Laura looked like till I got her home and in a fine little dress. You wear hospital night gowns too unless you want to buy Open down the front ones. I wore the hospital gowns till I got home and then took

four old gowns I didn't
mind spoiling and cut
slits over the breasts
about ten inches long
and bound them with
bias binding. They look
neat enough and are
all that is necessary — 2
late heavy gowns. I do
hope you can nurse
your baby — It is the
greatest feeling to feel
you have brought the
little thing into existence
and have nourished it
entirely from your own
body — It is easier than
bottles, too, a whole lot—

aside from sentiment and
makes little oases of
rest in a busy day —
You just have to sit
still twenty or more
minutes every 3 hours.
I started in feeding
Laura every 3 hours at
hospital and it is lots
better than every 2 hours.
Gives you more liberty
and doesn't hurt the
baby. It is all habit
any way.
The hardest part to
me has been looking
so sloppy — You know
you will never be th

same shape again and I am so big and fat. Simply don't wear a thing I ever had before and I never had any breasts to speak of - now they are large and I weigh 30 pounds more than when we were married - Of course I am wonderfully well - But 168 is some weight!

You want to know if I ate meat during the last months. Well, I did my best not to but I do love it so, that I -

broke once a few times
but not often. Ate
Chicken and fish right
along, though. I ate lots
of rice & tapioca and
<u>Scads</u> of fruit, it being
fruit time.
I should say you have
your trousseau well along.
I didn't make my nighties.
My sister in law gave
me 4 Arnold. Knit ones,
they are fine. You
don't iron them — 50¢ a
piece. It is a good
scheme to make things
big. Laura has out
grown her two dearest —
little dresses —

They are put away for
little brother — that doesn't
mean little brother is
on the way that I
know of. Have some
good dope fr present
that if you care to
know something harmless
& very simple — I don't
want another till Laura
is on her feet, for
her sake.
Oh yes — I have barron
coats for Laura for
nights. They help keep
her from getting so
wet & I change it
when I change her dids.

just outing flannel (15¢)
Cut 3/4 yard long + dart
so it is shaped like this
and pin around.
I have 4. the
top is bound with bias
binding so there is no
ridge to hurt her, like
a bulky hem would.
You will get a lot of
presents so don't worry
about the little fancy
things. Laura got 8 or 10
pairs of booties but
you can't have too
many. She got about
100 presents — I never
heard of such a thing —

189

Laura got so many sacks.
Etc. Mamma gave her
the basket I am enclosing
the cut. It was ordered
from Lamson Bros. (Toledo)
Catalog and holds all the
toilet articles in the top
and her dresses, shirts, etc
below. Just fine.
You don't take one thing
to the hospital, at least I
didn't, but your comb, +
tooth brush. Mamma brought
me the things to take
Laura home in + I had
to wear home what I wore
down as I was too big
for anything else. I have
a sleeping bag for Laura

like the enclosed and it is
all she ever wears out
doors in her sled -
Mamma was going to
get her a nice coat but
I said whats the use -
I feel her little feet are
snug & warm in this. It
is eider down. You could
make one. This one was
bought at Besta for about
$3.75. My cousin gave it
to me. I tell you you
don't know what you are
going to need till the
baby is here. And I
don't believe in getting
things like the crib, carriage
etc before hand. Too often
the first baby doesn't stay

in the world very long – I never got one thing like that for Laura. Superstitions, perhaps. My brothers' step daughter sent down her buggy – had it all done over – Then my sister in law sent a brass crib which is never uncrated yet & has been here about 4 months. I bought a little cheap cradle at a store in Jamestown for $1.75. It has good springs. I intend to enamel it white if I ever get a chance. It is just varnished. We put two pillows in it for a mattress. I like it so

it is so easy to move.
I have Laura as far away
as possible when we go
to bed. Then when she
wakes for her night feed
(some times not till six
a.m.) I haul the cradle
over beside the bed - take
Laura in the bath room &
dry her and then nurse
her in bed. She goes to
sleep at it + then I
land her over into her
Cradle generally without
her knowledge. Some times
she yells, though - last
night was one of those
times & I landed her back
+ fed her some more.

I didn't get a bassenette. They
are a needless expense as
the baby grows so fast.
I would get the carriage
as soon as possible after
you come home as it is
a grand good way to get
the baby to sleep when
all other means fail - Just
walk around the block &
the baby (mine did) goes
to sleep & she slept 5
hours at a stretch out
doors but never in doors.
Oh yes, about the breasts -
I painted the nipples night
& mornings with glycerine &
tannin the last two weeks
& had no trouble - It is
put up all ready by druggists.

Dear Roberts —

The enclosed Cradle is like mine only costs more. this

The doctor told me to use it and said if the nipples got sore it was more than having a baby — mine hurt a little one day & they put castor oil on, at the hospital. It is very healing. Gee whiz! I could talk for hours and am so glad if any thing I tell you is any help. It is evening now and Craig got the water thawed out — the temperature has riz. It was 16° below yesterday & I don't know what last night & today it went away up to 18° above! Write soon and keep me posted — I am so interested — Lots of love to you both — Yours, Dell.

JANUARY 1917

Jan. 9th — 1917

Dear Pearl — This is the second
time I have written 1917 so
you can see what a busy
letter writer I am but I do
feel badly that I am so
slow in thanking you for
the perfectly dear pins you
sent Laura. They are simply
too sweet for words and
her first pair so you can
imagine how they are
appreciated. Mother Pierce
writes that she has some
for her, too, and I am so
glad. The reason I am so slow
on my acknowledgments is that
Alice got sick just before
Christmas and I have been cook,
etc ever since — We are going
to do without her now as I
find I am as strong as ever
and able to do the work if
I only had time. Things have
to get slighted, though, as
Laura is the most important

and requires some one near. I wouldn't leave her for long at a time for any thing as the baby of friends of mine turned on his face and was smothered last month and he was just a little older than Laura. He was on the porch taking his nap. Laura is good as gold now - getting cuter every day and blowing bubbles till she is soaked to the skin.

I am so glad you liked the things I sent you. The picture is of Sherman and they are getting scarce on account of the war. I do hope they will make more. The dress, I know is awfully big but it is good to have some big ones. Laura's first are getting very snug now. I made yours just like one of Laura's and she has hers on today - It is just about right now

I am getting anxious to make her some more as she gets cuter and shows them off better. When they are so little it doesn't much matter what they have on. My! what a lot of fun you have ahead of you — Pearl, I actually don't care how soon I have another! They are so perfectly darling. Some times I think I don't want another when Laura has yowled half the night but she is really better than most and getting better all the time. At first she had colic or something some times but now she is good all day and I feel as if the worst is over. You wait till yours is actually here and Will can't help but get enthused over his nearest relative.

Laura is beginning to look more
like Craig and is just like his
baby pictures — her eyes are exactly
like his and her mouth too. Her
hair was black but is getting
lighter every day. The new hair
in under is golden.

Well, I must get lunch for
these people and nurse
Laura — her meals always
conflict with ours but I
should worry.

Do write and tell me all
your feelings — They interest me.
You should read "Diary of an
Expectant Mother" commenced in
Jan. Pictorial Review — She does
feel so much like I did —
When is your date? Do you
know?
                Lots of love —
                    Your Sister,
Love to Will.   Dee.

MAY 1917

Thursday Eve May 31 —

dear Pearl —

I am so lonesome
tonight I can taste it.
Mamma went home
yesterday and I miss
her just horribly — and
tonight Craig had to go
to an important — business
meeting at Wilkie — 20
miles away — I have
got Laura to bed and
am alone — the cook
sleeps in the house though
she cooks in the car
which stands about 50 feet
from the house. It keeps the
heat, odors etc out of the
house and is a lot easier
for me to keep the
house clean than as if
I had five, six or more
men tramping in three —

times a day from field and
barn. I are busy all day
as it is and tonight
have some back ache. Laura
is getting so heavy and I
lift her a good deal.
when she holds up her
little arms I just cant help
taking her. She weighs over
18 pounds and is such a
wiggler. Just you wait till
your young man is nearly
9 months old! Ill bet he
will be trying to stand
up — and Laura cant even
crawl though she gets on
her stomach and does a
kind of Australian Crawl.
Today she got about two
feet from her starting point.

She really tries to talk
though and says "Bye
Bye" and Papa.
I feel so badly not
to have written you
before but I suppose
Mother Pierce told you
all about our tribulations
with the cook and
the one we have now
is a good cook
but doesn't expect to
do any thing else. Well, you
know there are a good
many other things to do in
running a house beside
getting the meals, though
that is a big item. She
comes over to the house from
the car forty times a day
(no less) and hauls up a
chair and sits down and

watches me do whatever I
am doing. It certainly gets
me crazy. Craig has a boil
on the back of his neck
and some uncanny instinct
tells her whenever I am
going to dress it. I haven't
done it once without an
audience. I don't say a word,
though. I fired the other
cook and made poor Craig
so much trouble getting
another that I will put
up with most any thing
now and never cheep.
How are you getting along
with taking care of Richard?
Don't you find it eats into
your time very much. But
as I say to Mamma, they
are so worth while, one

can't keep it. I don't
mind not going any
place — the time will
soon be past when
the little things are so
dependent. Laura just
dotes on her parents.
Pats our cheeks and
holds out her arms.
I think abmt you
so much and wonder
if you are having
problems. You have
probably found out you
can't allow yourself any
emotions and nurse your
baby — nervousness, excitement,
etc seem to affect the
baby more than your food.
I give Laura malted milk
at 9, 12 + 3 now and
nurse her at six night
and morning and wherever

she wakes in the night.
I would like to keep that
up all summer if my
milk keeps worth anything
but if I wean her entirely
I will change gradually to
cows milk as we have a
cow now. I gave her two
teaspoonsful of egg yesterday
for a starter and she
liked it. Holt says start
about nine months on egg,
Etc. I suppose you use
Holt's Book. I couldn't do
without it though there are
lots of times I wish he
were more explicit

We go out in the automobile
a lot now that the roads
are good and Laura either

sleeps or sings. She
is good all the time
we are out and we
are often out several
hours.

Did Mamma tell Mother
Pierce about the Wrights
misfortune? The Keystone
Wrights, I mean. Newton
the older boy (Marian's
brother) died of diphtheria
last month and Martin
has it. Marian's husband
has been made manager of
the Hotel Athenaeum — Isn't
that fine?

My but I was glad to get
your letter telling all about
how everything happened. You
were lucky your water broke
so painlessly, I had a
frightful pain when mine
broke. It all came in a
flood and soaked the floor,

bed, and every thing around.
I didn't have any pulleys
to pull. My nurse was so
sure I didn't know any
thing that she wouldn't
believe I was very far
along so I nearly didn't even
have the doctor in time. I
get mad when I think of
it for most of the time I
was alone in the dark. She
kept telling me I could go
to sleep if I would — was
so sure I was only starting
when I was real finishing.
I never would have her
again but I guess she
learned a lesson — was
scared nearly to death at
the last for fear she would
have to deliver me. Well, Pearl,
I must close so I have to go to bed early
with this back (I am unwell thank goodness)
Please write soon + dont skip a thing. I
want to know every single thing — Lovingly, Dete.

207

MAY 1919

Drumheller, Alta.
Box 60.

Dear Pearl.

It has been so long
since your last letter and
so much has happened there
is no use in my trying
to tell you reasons for
not writing - you can imagine
yourself how busy you would
be if you were doing
all your own work and
moving - Then to move
into a house such as
this was and still is -
I can't describe it for
you never lived this way and
can't imagine it - no water in
the house, every drop has to
be carried from the wind
mill and all to be emptied
again, coal fires, coal to
carry and ashes to empty,
oil lamps, all such things
and worst of all the outside
toilet away off from the
house, almost an impossibility
in bad weather.

On top of this, the baby has
been bad ever since we came
out here. Whines all day
long till I am ready to
jump over the moon. Also
she had such a cold and
the matter just ran out of
her poor little eyes. Laura
also had it and a bad
cough besides and ear ache
which was simply fierce.
I had the grippe and am
just beginning to feel better.
Coughed at night till I
kept everybody awake and
nearly split my throat.
Mamma had it too but not
so bad. Only Craig escaped
and he is usually the
ring leader.
The day we came out here
(a month ago) was the last
nice day for some time.
It snowed the next day and
we were shut in and no

mail or any thing for
days – have out of coal,
butter and so on – then
Mrs Edwards, our cook,
left and I had to
cook four meals before
the new one got here –
meals for the men I
mean – Of course I get
all our meals in the
house here – Mrs E. is
expecting June 18th & I
didn't blame her for
wanting to go – She is
living in a little 12 × 12
shack away off ten miles from
here and was worrying about
having her baby so I told
her to come here and have
it and she is coming. I
wrote and asked my nurse
to come and take care of
her and she says she will
so we will have a house
full for a while next
month – There is so much
to do in the house in the
mean time it is appalling and
we are so held up by the weather

It was beautiful for a While and Craig got the Wheat all in but one more days work when the first day May it started to snow and we had the worst blizzard I ever remember seeing. It snowed two days + nights and then we had one nice day and a little thaw but last night it turned in again and made up for lost time — I hope there will be some pictures good enough to send. the boys took a lot yesterday. The drifts are over the top of the fences (5 foot fences) — you walk through one yard + step over the clothes line the snow is just a few inches below it. Really you would hardly believe it if you didn't see it + I do hope there are some good pictures to remember it by.

This is awful coming
right now when all the
farmers are seeding
And there is so much
to do around here it
makes your head
swim. We are living
in a kind of a
muddle ever since we
got here, held up in
every thing that has
to be done. The walls
were so awful I could
not live with them
so we have been

doing them in Muresco — But
even so many places the
plaster is off & of course
they will all have to
be done over. Then the
roof leaks & the newly
painted walls & ceilings
are getting streaked. But
I would have gone crazy
to have lived with them
as they were — bright blue &
salmon pink calcimine —

We have the whole down stairs in buff and gray and it is very restful and pretty. As soon as we can get the lumber hauled and a carpenter, we will have the up stairs finished — some more windows cut, partitions, etc., then the plasterers and then life will begin to assume a rosier hue. At present we are jammed into a little tunnel 6½ by 9, Craig, the baby & I. Mamma is in another similar coop, & Laura in the living room. When we get fixed right we will have two lovely big bed rooms up stairs & one small one. The tunnel will be an emergency guest room & Mamma's coop (a bright little spot with two windows) will be Craig's office. I must close. It is late & I could talk all night but believe me I'm tired when night comes. Write soon. Love to all. Yours—

NOTES

CHAPTER ONE

1. Cole 47
2. Bell 10
3. Monto 2
4. "ACP Journals" 7 Sep 1921
5. "ACP Journals" 27 Aug 1923
6. Cole 2
7. Langford 25
8. Vox Discipuli 1935–1936: 59
9. Bell 12
10. Bell 12
11. Rea 148
12. Bell 114
13. Bell 114
14. Bell 92
15. Cole 52
16. "ACP Journals" 5 Jun 1925
17. "ACP Journals" 4–8 Nov 1940
18. "ACP Journals" 16 Nov 1942
19. "Frontier Town"
20. Conover Interviews
21. Conover Interviews
22. Conover Interviews
23. Conover Interviews
24. 10 January 1929: 1
25. *The Drumheller Mail* 10 January 1929: 1
26. *The Drumheller Mail* 10 January 1929: 1
27. "ACP Journals" 10 Jan 1929
28. Conover Interviews
29. Rea 133
30. Rea 98
31. Monto 37
32. Bell 14
33. Conover Interviews
34. Conover Interviews
35. Conover Interviews
36. Conover Interviews
37. *The Acatec* 1938–1939: 5, 15

38. Conover Interviews
39. Penley Interview
40. *The Acatec* 1937–1938: 154
41. Penley Interview
42. *The Western Mirror* 2.6 [18 January 1937]: 6
43. Conover Interviews
44. Havighurst 82
45. Havighurst 82
46. Havighurst 83–4
47. Havighurst 82
48. "ACP Journals" 13 Dec 1937
49. "ACP Journals" 25 Nov 1919
50. Havighurst 82
51. Conover Interviews
52. Penley Interview
53. Conover Interviews
54. Conover Interviews
55. *The Acatec* 1937–1938: 155, 159
56. *The Western Mirror* 2.7 [25 January 1937]: 1
57. Penley Interview
58. *The Acatec* 1938–39: 78
59. *The Acatec* 1937–38: 19
60. *The Acatec* 1937–38: 23
61. Conover Interviews
62. Penley Interview
63. Bell 13
64. Monto 42
65. Conover Interviews
66. Conover Interviews
67. Conover Interviews
68. Conover Interviews
69. Conover Interviews
70. Conover Interviews
71. Conover Interviews
72. Conover Interviews
73. Conover Interviews
74. Conover Interviews
75. Conover Interviews

Chapter Two

1. Branton 3
2. Branton 12
3. Branton 39
4. *Catalogue 1902–03* 18
5. *Catalogue 1902–03* 18
6. *Catalogue 1902–03* 18
7. *Catalogue 1902–03* 6
8. *Catalogue 1902–03* 7
9. *Catalogue 1898–99* 36; *Catalogue 1899–1900* 35; *Catalogue 1900–01* 30;
   Catalogue 1902–03 23
10. *Catalogue 1907–08* 64
11. *Catalogue 1902–03* 7
12. *Catalogue 1902–03* 8
13. *Catalogue 1902–03* 19
14. *Catalogue 1902–03* 17
15. *Catalogue 1902–03* 19
16. *Catalogue 1902–03* 19
17. *Catalogue 1902–03* 20
18. *Catalogue 1902–03* 18
19. *Catalogue 1902–03* 18
20. *Catalogue 1902–03* 18
21. MAM 2 Apr 1957
22. Hayward 23 Sept [1916]
23. A. A. Moore 9 Sept 1916
24. Sipprell n.d. [10 Sept 1916]
25. MAM n.d. [Nov 1916]
26. MAM 9 Jan 1917
27. MAM 9 Jan 1917
28. MAM n.d. [4 Oct 1916]
29. MAM n.d. [4 Oct 1916]
30. MAM n.d. [4 Oct 1916]
31. MAM n.d. [4 Oct 1916]
32. MAM n.d. [4 Oct 1916]
33. MAM n.d. [Nov 1916]
34. MAM n.d. [Nov 1916]
35. MAM n.d. [Nov 1916]
36. MAM 9 Jan 1917
37. Quoted in Craik 73
38. MAM 4 Oct 1916
39. MAM 4 Oct 1916

40. MAM n.d. [late Oct 1916]
41. MAM n.d. [late Oct 1916]
42. MAM n.d. [late Oct 1916]
43. MAM n.d. [Nov 1916]
44. MAM May 1919
45. MAM May 1919
46. MAM May 1919
47. Pierce family photographs
48. McNamara
49. "ACP Journals" 20–25 Mar 1920
50. "ACP Journals" 31 Mar 1920
51. "ACP Journals" 1 Apr 1920
52. "ACP Journals" 5, 8, 17 Apr 1920
53. MAM May 1919
54. "ACP Journals" 27 Aug 1921
55. "ACP Journals" 22 Oct 1921
56. "ACP Journals" 28 Jul 1923
57. "ACP Journals" 2 Nov 1923
58. "ACP Journals" 15 Mar 1924
59. "ACP Journals" 6–17 Apr 1924
60. "ACP Journals" 13 Apr 1924
61. "ACP Journals" 10 May 1924
62. "ACP Journals" 16 May 1924
63. "ACP Journals" 21 Aug 1925
64. "ACP Journals" 18 Oct 1925
65. "ACP Journals" 30 Mar 1926
66. "ACP Journals" 30 Oct 1926
67. Clark 1
68. Clark 3
69. "ACP Journals" 10 Jun 1938; Pierce photographs
70. Warner Interview
71. Moore Interview
72. MAM May 1919

CHAPTER THREE

1. MacEwan 3
2. Conover and Moore Interviews
3. Conover Interviews
4. Conover Interviews
5. Havighurst 3
6. Palmer 53

7. Palmer 127

8. Palmer 892

9. Palmer 509

10. *The Albertan* 22 April 1955: 16

11. *Lehigh Register* 88

12. *Lehigh Register* 88–9

13. *Farming in Canada* n.d.: 14

14. *SRM News* 8.5 (15 August 1966): 4

15. Conover Interview

16. *Nor'-West Farmer* 8

17. Moore interview

18. unidentified source

19. "ACP Journals" 16 Dec 1954

20. *Camrose Canadian* 17

21. *Camrose Canadian* 22

22. McGuinness 123

23. Schmidt 22

24. McGuinness 124

25. "ACP Journals" 29 May 1926

26. "ACP Journals" 8 Jun 1926

27. "ACP Journals" 3 Apr 1933

28. McGuinness 126

29. The Camrose Canadian 27 April 1955: 17

30. unidentified news clipping

31. unidentified news clipping

32. unidentified news clipping

33. Priestley letter to ACP

34. Nesbitt 1

35. Conover Interviews

36. Conover Interviews

37. Warner interview

38. Conover Interviews

39. Conover Interviews

40. Conover Interviews

41. Conover Interviews

42. "ACP Journals" 25 Nov 1919

43. "ACP Journals" 19 Jan 1952

CHAPTER FOUR

1. Letter from Jet n.d. [8 Sept 1916]

2. "ACP Journals" 22 Jun 1921

3. Conover Interviews
4. Conover Interviews
5. Conover Interviews
6. Conover Interviews
7. Conover Interviews
8. Conover Interviews
9. Conover Interviews
10. Conover Interviews
11. Warner Interview
12. "ACP Journals" 9 Dec 1930
13. Conover Interviews
14. "ACP Journals" Dec 1930
15. "ACP Journals" 14 Dec 1930
16. "ACP Journals" 25 Dec 1930
17. Conover Interviews
18. Perkins letter 1930
19. n.d. [#2 early Jan 1928]
20. n.d. [#1 early Jan 1928]
21. n.d. [#2 early Jan 1928]
22. n.d. [#3 early Jan 1928]
23. n.d. [#1 early Jan 1928]
24. n.d. [#2 early Jan 1928]
25. n.d. [#2 early Jan 1928]
26. n.d. [#3 early Jan 1928]
27. Conover Interviews
28. Conover Interviews
29. Conover Interviews
30. Conover Interviews

CHAPTER FIVE

1. MAM Letter to Pearl Pierce, May 1919
2. "ACP Journals" 26 Jul 1920
3. "ACP Journals" 1920
4. "ACP Journals" 25 Feb 1924
5. Leman 27
6. Penley Interview
7. *The Acatec* 1936–1937: 15
8. "ACP Journals" 1935–1938
9. "ACP Journals" 6 Aug 1939
10. *The Acatec* 1937–1938: 33
11. Provincial Institute *Eighteenth Annual Announcement*: 25

12. Provincial Institute *Eighteenth Annual Announcement*: 25
13. *The Mirror* 3.10: 5
14. *The Mirror* 1.3: 4
15. Conover Interviews
16. "ACP Journals" 28 Jul 1940
17. "ACP Journals" 18 Aug 1940
18. "ACP Journals" 19 Aug 1940
19. "ACP Journals" 21 Aug 1940
20. unidentified source
21. "ACP Journals" 21 Aug 1940
22. "ACP Journals" 1940
23. "ACP Journals" 9 Sep 1940
24. "ACP Journals" 7 Oct 1940
25. "ACP Journals" 22 Nov 1940
26. "ACP Journals" 28 Nov 1940
27. "ACP Journals" 1941-44
28. Conover Interviews

CHAPTER SIX

1. Conover Interviews
2. *The Acatec* 1937–38: 33
3. *Vox Discipuli* 1935–36
4. *The Acatec* 1936–1937: 50
5. Penley Interview
6. Conover Interviews
7. *The Mirror* 3.1: 5
8. *The Mirror* 2.11: 2
9. *The Acatec* 1937–1938
10. *The Mirror* 3.13: 8
11. *The Mirror* 3.26: 1
12. *The Mirror* 3.9: 1
13. *The Mirror* 3.8: 4
14. *The Acatec* 1937–1938: 112
15. *The Mirror* 3.12: 5
16. *Vox Discipuli* 1935–1936: 82
17. *The Mirror* 3.13: 8
18. *The Mirror* 3.14: 5
19. Conover Interviews
20. *The Mirror* 3.18: 4
21. *The Mirror* 3.19: 7
22. Leman 72–81
23. "ACP Journals" 15 Aug 1939

24. Conover Interviews
25. "ACP Journals" 1939
26. "ACP Journals" 5 Feb 1940
27. "ACP Journals" 7 Feb 1940
28. "ACP Journals" 23 Feb 1940
29. *Bulletin* 184
30. *The Acatec* 1936-1937: 15
31. "ACP Journals" 1941-1942
32. "ACP Journals" 1942
33. "ACP Journals" 1942
34. "ACP Journals" 1944
35. "ACP Journals" 24 Jun 1944
36. "ACP Journals" 25 Jun 1944
37. "ACP Journals" 26 Jul 1944
38. "ACP Journals"
39. "ACP Journals" 4 Nov 1944

CHAPTER SEVEN

1. Conover Interviews
2. "ACP Journals" 16 Dec 1939
3. "ACP Journals" 15 Dec 1939
4. "ACP Journals" 22 Oct 1921
5. Leman 83-4
6. Conover Interviews
7. Leman 84
8. Conover Interviews
9. Conover Interviews
10. "ACP Journals" 18 Jul 1930
11. Conover Interviews
12. Conover Interviews
13. "ACP Journals" 3 May 1930
14. Conover Interviews
15. "ACP Journals" 3 May 1930
16. *The Acatec* 1937–1938: 53
17. Conover Interviews
18. Conover Interviews
19. Conover Interviews
20. *The Acatec* 1938–1939: 33
21. Conover Interviews
22. Conover Interviews
23. Conover Interviews

24. "ACP Journals" 9 Mar 1942
25. Conover Interviews
26. "ACP Journals"
27. Penley Interview
28. Penley Interview
29. *The Acatec* 1937–1938: 103
30. *The Acatec* 1937–1938: 112
31. *The Acatec* 1937–1938: 112
32. "ACP Journals" 26 May 1939
33. Conover Interviews
34. Conover Interviews
35. Conover Interviews
36. "ACP Journals" 9 Feb 1941
37. "ACP Journals" 7 Mar 1942
38. Conover Interviews
39. Conover Interviews
40. "ACP Journals" 26 Dec 1950 [in 1951 vol]
41. "ACP Journals" 23 Apr 1951
42. "ACP Journals" 30 Apr 1951
43. "ACP Journals" 21 May 1951
44. "ACP Journals" 4 Aug 1951
45. Leman 84
46. Conover Interviews
47. Conover Interviews
48. Conover Interviews
49. Conover Interviews
50. Conover Interviews

BIBLIOGRAPHY AND REFERENCES

The Acatec. Western Canada High School, Calgary AB. 1936/37–1938/39.

Bell, Edward. *Social Classes and Social Credit in Alberta.* Montreal: Queen's University Press, 1993.

Branton, Harriet K. "'Dear Old Sem': The Story of the Washington Female Seminary 1836–1948." Washington, PA: Washington County Historical Society.

The Camrose Canadian 27 April 1955: 17. Pierce Family Fonds, Glenbow Museum.

Clark, Henrietta Pierce. "The A. Craig Pierce Family." ca. 1979–86. Pierce Family Fonds, Glenbow Museum.

Cole, Catherine C., and Judy Larmour. *Many and Remarkable: The Story of the Alberta Women's Institutes.* Edmonton, AB: Alberta Women's Institutes, 1997.

The College of Washington Bulletin 1940. Pullman, WA: Washington State University.

Conover, Mary Pierce. Interviews. 19 July 1996; 22–23 November 1999; June–July 2002.

Craik, Jennifer. *The Face of Fashion: Cultural Studies in Fashion.* New York: Routledge, 1994.

The Drumheller Mail 10 January 1929: 1. Pierce Family Fonds, Glenbow Museum.

Eighteenth Annual Announcement. 1937–1938. Calgary, AB: Provincial Institute of Technology and Art.

The Epitome. MCMVII [1908]. Published by the Junior Class of Lehigh University. Volume Thirty-One. Lehigh, PA.

Farming in Canada. Union Tractor & Harvester Co., Ltd. n.d. Pierce Family Fonds, Glenbow Museum.

"Frontier Town to Modern City: Calgary 1895–1946." *Calgary and Southern Alberta*. The Applied History Research Group, The University of Calgary, 1997. Web. 16 August 2003. <http://www.ucalgary.ca/applied_history/tutor/calgary/calgary1895.html>.

Havighurst, Walter E. *From Six at First: A History of Phi Delta Theta, 1848–1973*. Menasha, WI: George Banta, 1975.

Hayward, Molly. Letter to MAM. 23 September [1916]. Pierce Family Fonds, Glenbow Museum.

Jet [surname unknown]. Letter to MAM. n.d. [8 September 1916]. Pierce Family Fonds, Glenbow Museum.

Langford, Nanci L. *Politics, Pitchforks and Pickle Jars: 75 Years of Organized Farm Women in Alberta*. Calgary, AB: Detselig Enterprises, 1997.

Lehigh University Register 1904–1905. Lehigh PA.

Leman, Kevin. T*he Birth Order Book: Why You Are the Way You Are*. Old Tappan, NJ: Revell, 1984.

MacEwan, Grant. "Trees are Living Monuments to Pioneer Farmer." *Western Weekly* 2 Jan. 1963: 3. Pierce Family Fonds, Glenbow Museum.

McGuinness, Fred. "Tying Down the Prairie Topsoil." *The Reader's Digest* June 1976: 122–127. Pierce Family Fonds, Glenbow Museum.

McNamara, Robert M. "Syphilis." *eMedicine from WebMD*. Web. 9 July 2000. <http://emedicine.com/>.

Monto, Tom. *The United Farmers of Alberta: A Movement, a Government*. Edmonton, AB: Crang Publishing, 1989.

Moore, Arthur Allison. Letter to MAM. 9 September 1916. Pierce Family Fonds, Glenbow Museum.

Moore, James Gillette. Interview. 4 November 1999.

Nesbitt, Leonard D. "Aid for Canada's Soldiers." *The Calgary Herald*, magazine section. 22 March 1941. Pierce Family Fonds, Glenbow Museum.

The Nor'-West Farmer October 1935:8. Pierce Family Fonds, Glenbow Museum.

Palmer, Walter Benjamin. *The History of the Phi Delta Theta Fraternity.* Menasha, WI: George Banta, 1906.

Penley, Ken. Interview. 28 June 1999.

Perkins, L. M. Letter to Laura. n.d. [23 December 1930]. Pierce Family Fonds, Glenbow Museum.

Pierce, A. Craig. "ACP Journals." 1919–1955. Pierce Family Fonds, Glenbow Museum.

———. Postcard to MAM. 7 May 1915. Pierce Family Fonds, Glenbow Museum.

Pierce, Laura Allison. Letters to MAM. n.d. [early Jan. 1928]. Pierce Family Fonds, Glenbow Museum.

Pierce, Margaret Adele (Moore). Letters to Pearl: n.d. [4 October 1916]; n.d. [late October 1916]; n.d. [November-December 1916]; 9 January 1917; 31 May [1917]; n.d. [May 1919]; 2 April 1957. Pierce Family Fonds, Glenbow Museum.

———. Letters to Laura. n.d. [early Jan. 1928]. Pierce Family Fonds, Glenbow Museum.

Pierce Family Fonds: Laura Pierce's "Baby's Year Book." Glenbow Museum.

Pierce family news clippings, Glenbow Museum.

Pierce family photographs, Glenbow Museum.

Rea, J. E. *T. A. Crerar: A Political Life.* Montreal: McGill-Queen's University Press, 1997.

Schmidt, John. *The Calgary Herald* Tuesday, August 8, 1967: 22. Pierce Family Fonds, Glenbow Museum.

Sipprell, Lucy Allen. Letter to MAM. n.d. [10 September 1916]. Pierce Family Fonds, Glenbow Museum.

SRM News 8.5 (15 August 1966). Pierce Family Fonds, Glenbow Museum.

Vox Discipuli. Calgary, AB: Western Canada High School. 1935–36.

Warner, Jane Moore. Interview. 19 December 1997.

Warner, Klaran. E-mail to author. 9 July 2000.

Washington Seminary: 1907–08. Washington, PA: Citizens Library.

Washington Seminary: Annual Catalogue 1901–1902. Washington, PA: Citizens Library.

Washington Seminary: Annual Catalogue 1902–1903. Washington, PA: Citizens Library.

Washington Seminary: Record of Students of 1898–99, with Prospectus for 1899–1900. Washington, PA: Citizens Library.

Washington Seminary: Record of Students of 1899–1900, with Prospectus for 1900–01. Washington, PA: Citizens Library.

The Western Mirror 1.1 (14 February 1936) – 4.25 (22 May 1939). Calgary, AB: Western Canada High School.

The Year Book 1934/35. Calgary, AB: Western Canada High School.